The Lunch Box Cookbook

Over 50 Fun and Delicious Recipes to Fill Your Lunch Box

By
BookSumo Press
All rights reserved

Published by
http://www.booksumo.com

Table of Contents

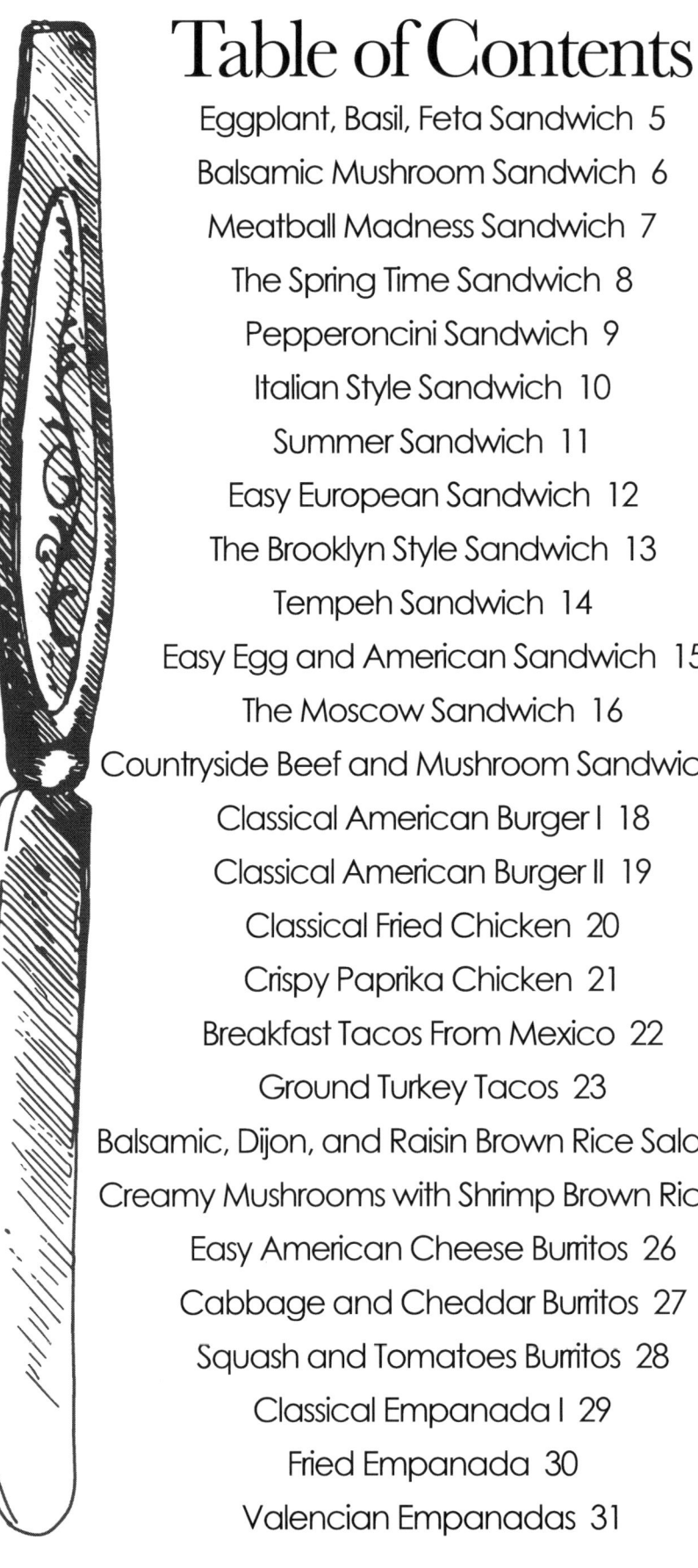

Eggplant, Basil, Feta Sandwich 5
Balsamic Mushroom Sandwich 6
Meatball Madness Sandwich 7
The Spring Time Sandwich 8
Pepperoncini Sandwich 9
Italian Style Sandwich 10
Summer Sandwich 11
Easy European Sandwich 12
The Brooklyn Style Sandwich 13
Tempeh Sandwich 14
Easy Egg and American Sandwich 15
The Moscow Sandwich 16
Countryside Beef and Mushroom Sandwich 17
Classical American Burger I 18
Classical American Burger II 19
Classical Fried Chicken 20
Crispy Paprika Chicken 21
Breakfast Tacos From Mexico 22
Ground Turkey Tacos 23
Balsamic, Dijon, and Raisin Brown Rice Salad 24
Creamy Mushrooms with Shrimp Brown Rice 25
Easy American Cheese Burritos 26
Cabbage and Cheddar Burritos 27
Squash and Tomatoes Burritos 28
Classical Empanada I 29
Fried Empanada 30
Valencian Empanadas 31

Cheddar, Chipotle, Bacon Sandwich 32
Romano, Basil, Chicken Sandiwch 33
Sourdough, Provolone, Pesto 34
Avocado, Turkey, Spinach, Ciabatta 35
Sesame Ramen Coleslaw 36
Broccoli Ramen Salad 37
Venetian Beef Ramen Stir-Fry 38
Natural Ramen Noodles 39
Cabbage Ramen Salad I 40
Ramen for College 41
Easy Ramen Soup 42
Cheesy Ramen 43
Cabbage Ramen Salad II 44
Jalapeno Lime Sirloin Taco 45
Swiss Chard and Onions Taco 46
Guacamole and Tomatoes Taco 47
Coleslaw Taco 48
Corn and Beef Taco 49
Shrimp and Cilantro Taco 50
Teriyaki Steak Tacos 51
Cheddar Beef Taco 52
Beans and White Rice Taco 53
Tempeh & Veggie Vegetarian Tacos 54
Soft and Hard Shell Tacos 55
Oriental Coleslaw 56
Garden Party Coleslaw 57
Sunflower Coleslaw 58
Famous New England Coleslaw 59

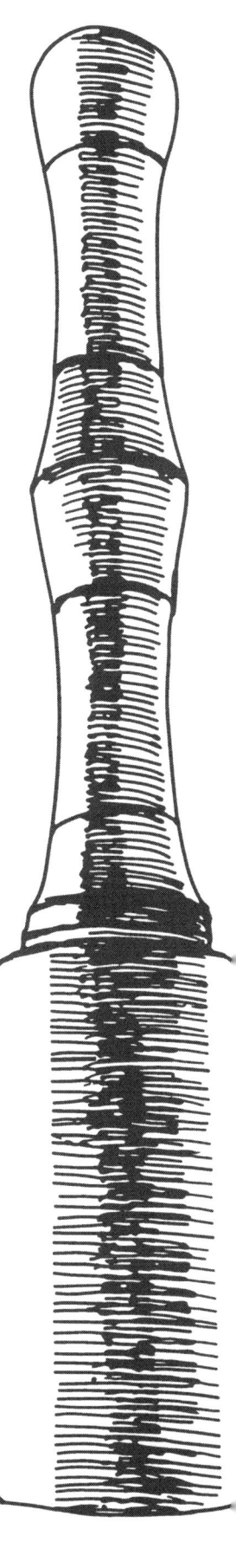

Chocolate Yogurt Cookies 60
New England Apple Cookies 61
Chewy Cookies 101 62
Quesadillas Tegucigalpa Style 63
Turkey Quesadillas 64
American Quesadillas 65
Brightly Flavored Quesadillas 66
Milanese Quesadillas 67
Cajun Burgers with Lemon Sauce 68
Kalamata Feta Burgers 69
Hot Iceberg Chicken Burgers 70
Sesame Burgers 71
Feta Spinach Burgers 72
Bell Artichoke Burgers 73
Fathia's Favorite 74
Chili Corn Burgers 75
Italian Balsamic Mushroom Burger 76
Birdie Burgers 77

Eggplant Basil, Feta Sandwich

Prep Time: 20 mins
Total Time: 30 mins

Servings per Recipe: 2
Calories	802 kcal
Fat	39.5 g
Carbohydrates	91.3g
Protein	23.8 g
Cholesterol	44 mg
Sodium	1460 mg

Ingredients

- 1 small eggplant, halved and sliced
- 1 tbsp olive oil, or as needed
- 1/4 C. mayonnaise
- 2 cloves garlic, minced
- 2 (6 inch) French sandwich rolls
- 1 small tomato, sliced
- 1/2 C. crumbled feta cheese
- 1/4 C. minced fresh basil leaves

Directions

1. Turn on your broiler to low if possible.
2. Get a bowl, mix: garlic and mayo.
3. Take your eggplant pieces and coat them with olive oil. Put them on a sheet for baking.
4. For 10 mins cook the eggplant in the broiler 6 inches from the heat.
5. Cut your French bread in half and toast it.
6. Spread a good amount of mayo and garlic mix on your bread and layer the following to form a sandwich: tomato, basil leaves, eggplant, and feta.
7. Enjoy.

BALSAMIC MUSHROOM Sandwich

🥣 Prep Time: 8 mins
🕐 Total Time: 20 mins

Servings per Recipe: 4
Calories   445 kcal
Fat   33.4 g
Carbohydrates   31.4g
Protein   7.8 g
Cholesterol   5 mg
Sodium   426 mg

Ingredients

2 cloves garlic, minced
6 tbsps olive oil
1/2 tsp dried thyme
2 tbsps balsamic vinegar
salt and pepper to taste
4 large Portobello mushroom caps
4 hamburger buns
1 tbsp capers

1/4 C. mayonnaise
1 tbsp capers, drained
1 large tomato, sliced
4 leaves lettuce

Directions

1. Preheat your broiler and set its rack so that it is near the heating source before doing anything else.
2. Get a bowl and mix: pepper, garlic, salt, olive oil, vinegar, and thyme.
3. Get a 2nd bowl, combine: mayo and capers.
4. Coat your mushrooms with half of the dressing.
5. Then toast the veggies for 5 mins under the broiler.
6. Flip the mushrooms after coating the opposite side with the remaining dressing.
7. Toast everything for 5 more mins.
8. Now also toast your bread.
9. Apply some mayo to the bread before layering a mushroom, some lettuce and tomato.
10. Enjoy.

Meatball Madness Sandwich

🥣 Prep Time: 20 mins
🕐 Total Time: 40 mins

Servings per Recipe: 4
Calories   781 kcal
Fat   31.9 g
Carbohydrates   78.2g
Protein   43.6 g
Cholesterol   141 mg
Sodium   1473 mg

Ingredients

- 1 lb ground beef
- 3/4 C. bread crumbs
- 2 tsps dried Italian seasoning
- 2 cloves garlic, minced
- 2 tbsps minced fresh parsley
- 2 tbsps grated Parmesan cheese
- 1 egg, beaten
- 1 French baguette
- 1 tbsp extra-virgin olive oil
- 1/2 tsp garlic powder
- 1 pinch salt, or to taste
- 1 (14 oz.) jar spaghetti sauce
- 4 slices provolone cheese

Directions

1. Set your oven to 350 degrees before doing anything else.
2. Get a bowl, combine: eggs, beef, parmesan, bread crumbs, parsley, garlic, and Italian seasoning.
3. Mold the mix into your preferred size of meatballs and cook them in the oven for 22 mins.
4. Now cut your bread and take out some of the inside so the meatballs fit better.
5. Toast the bread for 6 mins in the oven after coating it with some olive oil, salt, and garlic powder.
6. Get a saucepan and heat up your pasta sauce.
7. Add in your meatballs to the sauce after they are cooked and mix everything.
8. Put some meatballs into your bread and then toast the sandwich in the oven for 4 mins before serving.
9. Enjoy.

THE SPRING TIME
Sandwich

🥣 Prep Time: 25 mins
🕒 Total Time: 25 mins

Servings per Recipe: 4
Calories   811 kcal
Fat   56.1 g
Carbohydrates   29.6 g
Protein   46.3 g
Cholesterol   204 mg
Sodium   908 mg

Ingredients

- 1/2 C. mayonnaise
- 1/4 C. blue cheese dressing
- 8 slices multigrain bread
- 2 cooked chicken breasts, sliced
- 1 ripe avocado, sliced
- 8 slices cooked turkey bacon
- 2 hard-boiled eggs, minced
- 4 lettuce leaves

Directions

1. Get a bowl and mix the blue cheese with some mayo.
2. Coat your bread with 2 tbsps of this mix.
3. Place a quarter of your chicken breast on four pieces of bread.
4. Then layer the following on each piece: lettuce, avocado, hard-boiled egg, bacon, another piece of bread.
5. Enjoy with some blue cheese on the side for dipping.

Pepperoncini Sandwich

🥣 Prep Time: 10 mins
🕐 Total Time: 10 mins

Servings per Recipe: 1
Calories   496 kcal
Fat   32.5 g
Carbohydrates   46.3g
Protein   11.4 g
Cholesterol   32 mg
Sodium   1024 mg

Ingredients

2 thick slices whole wheat bread
2 tbsps cream cheese, softened
6 slices cucumber
2 tbsps alfalfa sprouts
1 tsp olive oil
1 tsp red vinegar
1 tomato, sliced

1 leaf lettuce
1 oz. pepperoncini, sliced
1/2 avocado, mashed

Directions

1. Layer one piece of bread with the following: 1 tbsp of cream cheese, alfalfa sprouts, oil and vinegar, cucumber pieces, tomatoes, pepperoncini, and lettuce.
2. Coat another piece of bread with avocado and form a sandwich.
3. Enjoy.

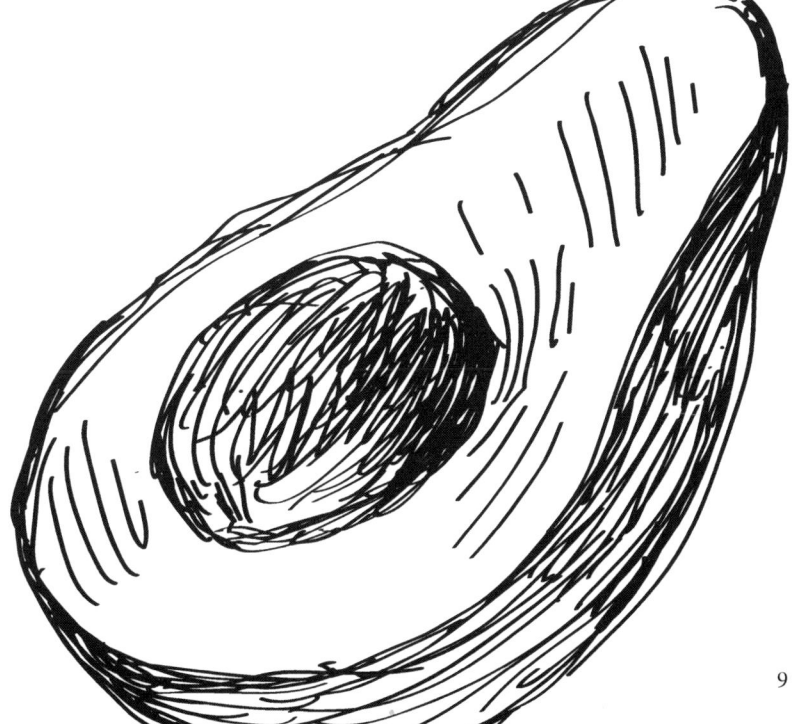

ITALIAN STYLE
Sandwich

🥣 Prep Time: 15 mins
🕒 Total Time: 15 mins

Servings per Recipe: 4
Calories   975 kcal
Fat   59.9 g
Carbohydrates   61.3g
Protein   46.2 g
Cholesterol   107 mg
Sodium   2790 mg

Ingredients

1 (1 lb) loaf fresh Italian bread
1/3 C. olive oil
1/3 C. grated Parmesan cheese
1 tbsp dried basil
1 tbsp dried oregano
8 oil-cured black olives, pitted and minced

8 pitted green olives, minced
1/4 lb thinly sliced beef salami
1/4 lb thinly sliced turkey
1/2 lb provolone cheese, sliced
1/4 lb mozzarella cheese, sliced

Directions

1. Cut your bread in half then coat one side with: olive oil, oregano, parmesan, and basil.
2. Add the following to the other piece: green olives, mozzarella, black olives, provolone, turkey and salami.
3. Form everything into a sandwich and divide it into multiple pieces.
4. Enjoy.

Summer Sandwich

Prep Time: 15 mins
Total Time: 20 mins

Servings per Recipe: 8
Calories   386 kcal
Fat   21.5 g
Carbohydrates   31.6 g
Protein   16.8 g
Cholesterol   40 mg
Sodium   738 mg

Ingredients

1 (1 lb) loaf ciabatta bread
3/4 C. pesto
8 oz. fontina cheese, sliced
2 ripe tomatoes, sliced

4 leaves butter lettuce

Directions

1. Turn on your oven's broiler to low if possible.
2. Cut your bread in half. Coat one side with some pesto then layer the following on the other side: tomato, and fontina cheese.
3. Place the pieces of bread which have cheese under the broiler until the cheese has melted.
4. Top this piece with some lettuce.
5. Form sandwiches then cut them in half for serving.
6. Enjoy.

EASY EUROPEAN
Sandwich

🥣 Prep Time: 15 mins
🕐 Total Time: 30 mins

Servings per Recipe: 25
Calories   233 kcal
Fat   12.9 g
Carbohydrates   21.9 g
Protein   7.7 g
Cholesterol   39 mg
Sodium   470 mg

Ingredients

1 (8 oz.) package cream cheese, softened
1/2 C. butter, softened
1 tbsp minced garlic
2 loaves French bread, sliced
1 lb sliced beef sausage

1 cucumber, sliced
3 medium tomatoes, sliced
1 hard-cooked egg, minced

Directions

1. Get a bowl, mix: garlic, butter, and cream cheese.
2. Coat a piece of bread with this mix.
3. Then layer the following on each bread piece: tomato, sausage, cucumber, egg.
4. Enjoy this sandwich open.

The Brooklyn Style Sandwich

🥣 Prep Time: 30 mins
🕐 Total Time: 45 mins

Servings per Recipe: 4
Calories   892 kcal
Fat   45.3 g
Carbohydrates   79.5g
Protein   42.7 g
Cholesterol   97 mg
Sodium   1604 mg

Ingredients

- 3 C. shredded cabbage
- 2 tbsps vegetable oil
- 2 tbsps apple cider vinegar
- 2 tbsps white sugar
- 1 tsp adobo seasoning
- 1 tsp ground black pepper
- 4 C. vegetable oil for frying
- 3 whole russet potatoes
- 8 thick slices Italian bread
- 1 lb sliced pastrami (divided)
- 4 slices provolone cheese
- 8 slices tomato

Directions

1. Get a bowl and combine evenly: black pepper, cabbage, adobo, veggie oil (2 tbsps), sugar, and vinegar.
2. Get a large pot and get your oil to 375 degrees then set your oven to 225 degrees before doing anything else.
3. Dice your potatoes into slices and fry them in the oil for 6 mins.
4. Now place the potatoes to the side.
5. For 6 mins toast your bread in the oven.
6. On 4 slices of bread layer: pastrami and cheese.
7. Now toast the pieces for 4 more mins to melt the cheese.
8. Layer the following on the pastrami: 2 tomato pieces, cabbage mix, fried potatoes, and another piece of toasted bread.
9. Enjoy.

TEMPEH Sandwich (Vegetarian Approved)

🥣 Prep Time: 10 mins
🕐 Total Time: 30 mins

Servings per Recipe: 4
Calories   392 kcal
Fat   24.8 g
Carbohydrates   24.4g
Protein   21.7 g
Cholesterol   28 mg
Sodium   551 mg

Ingredients

1 tbsp sesame oil
1 (8 oz.) package tempeh, sliced into thin strips
2 tbsps liquid amino acid supplement
1 tbsp sesame oil
1 small onion, thinly sliced
1 medium green bell pepper, thinly sliced
1 jalapeno pepper, sliced
2 pita breads, cut in half
soy mayonnaise
4 thin slices Swiss cheese

Directions

1. For 5 mins fry your tempeh in hot oil, add half of the amino's liquid, then cook everything for 2 more mins.
2. Flip all the tempeh pieces and continue frying them for another 2 mins.
3. Now add the rest of the amino's liquid and cook the mix for 2 more mins.
4. Place everything to the side.
5. Stir fry your jalapenos, onions, and green peppers for 6 mins with fresh oil in the same pan.
6. Coat each piece of pita with some mayo (1 tsp).
7. Then fill each piece with some onion mix, tempeh, and Swiss cheese.
8. For 2 mins toast the pita in a toaster oven or on the stove until the Swiss melts.
9. Enjoy.

Easy Egg and American Sandwich

🥣 Prep Time: 1 mins
🕐 Total Time: 5 mins

Servings per Recipe: 1
Calories   318 kcal
Fat   15.8 g
Carbohydrates   26.9 g
Protein   16.9 g
Cholesterol   214 mg
Sodium   839 mg

Ingredients

1 egg
1 tbsp milk
2 slices white bread
salt and pepper to taste (optional)

1 slice American cheese

Directions

1. Get a bowl, and mix: whisked eggs, salt, pepper, and milk.
2. Microwave the mix for 90 secs in the microwave with the highest power setting.
3. Simultaneously toast your bread slices then add your egg to the toasted bread.
4. Before forming a sandwich top the egg with a piece of cheese.
5. Now heat everything in the microwave for 30 more secs.
6. Enjoy.

Easy Egg and American Sandwich

MOSCOW
Sandwich

🥣 Prep Time: 4 mins
🕒 Total Time: 5 mins

Servings per Recipe: 1
Calories 535 kcal
Fat 28.8 g
Carbohydrates 38.7g
Protein 30.8 g
Cholesterol 88 mg
Sodium 2472 mg

Ingredients

2 slices American cheese
2 slices white bread, toasted
3 slices deli-style sliced turkey breast
2 tbsps Russian salad dressing

Directions

1. On one piece of toasted bread put 1 piece of cheese.
2. Now heat it in the microwave for 30 secs.
3. Layer some turkey on the cheese and on the remaining piece of bread coat it with some Russian dressing.
4. Form a sandwich and enjoy.

Countryside Beef and Mushroom Sandwich

 Prep Time: 25 mins
 Total Time: 7 hrs 45 mins

Servings per Recipe: 6
Calories   516 kcal
Fat   22.3 g
Carbohydrates   42.9 g
Protein   34.3 g
Cholesterol   78 mg
Sodium   635 mg

Ingredients

1 loaf hearty country bread, unsliced
3 tbsps vegetable oil, divided
1 (3 lb) boneless beef round steak, 2 inches thick
1 onion, thinly sliced
2 C. sliced fresh mushrooms
1 clove garlic, minced, or to taste
salt to taste
ground black pepper to taste
garlic salt to taste

Directions

1. Slice off a piece of bread from the loaf and keep it for later.
2. Now remove the inside center of the loaf.
3. This space is to be filled later.
4. Fry your steak in 1 tbsp of veggie oil for 6 mins per side then place the steak to the side.
5. Stir fry your mushrooms, onions, and garlic for 7 mins until the onions are see through in 2 more tbsps of veggie oil.
6. Fill the hollowed bread with: the mushrooms, onions, and steak.
7. Put the first piece of bread you sliced off earlier back on the loaf.
8. Now cover everything with foil.
9. Lay the bread in a casserole dish and place something heavy on top of it. Like a cast iron frying pan with jars of water in it.
10. For 7 hrs let the bread sit in the fridge with the pan on top of it.
11. When ready to serve, cut the sandwich into servings.
12. Enjoy.

CLASSICAL AMERICAN
Burger I

🥣 Prep Time: 5 mins
🕐 Total Time: 20 mins

Servings per Recipe: 8
Calories   229 kcal
Carbohydrates   3.5 g
Cholesterol   82 mg
Fat   18.2 g
Fiber   0.2 g
Protein   12.1 g
Sodium   247 mg

Ingredients

1 lb ground beef
1 slice bread, crumbled
1 egg
2 tbsps prepared mustard
3 tbsps Worcestershire sauce

garlic salt to taste
salt and pepper to taste

Directions

1. Take out a large bowl and mix beef, egg, Worcestershire sauce and mustard.
2. Now make 8 patties and also add some salt, pepper and garlic (salt according to your taste).
3. Now cook these patties in a skillet that is over medium heat for about 15 mins to reach the required tenderness.

Classical American Burger II (Spicy Chili Burger)

🥣 Prep Time: 15 mins
🕐 Total Time: 25 mins

Servings per Recipe: 8
Calories   232 kcal
Carbohydrates   1.1 g
Cholesterol   70 mg
Fat   16.4 g
Fiber   0.4 g
Protein   19.1 g
Sodium   67 mg

Ingredients

- 1 tsp ground cumin
- 2 tbsps chopped fresh cilantro
- 1 tsp crushed red pepper flakes
- 1 fresh habanero pepper, seeded and minced (optional)
- 1 small fresh poblano chile pepper, seeded and minced
- 2 fresh jalapeno peppers, seeded and minced
- 2 tsps minced garlic
- 2 lbs ground beef

Directions

1. Set grill or grilling plate at medium heat and put some oil before continuing.
2. Take out a large bowl and mix beef, jalapeno peppers, poblano pepper, garlic, red pepper flakes, cilantro, habanero pepper and cumin.
3. Make burger patties from this mixture and cook them on the heated grill for about 5 mins each side.
4. NOTE: If using a grilling plate then increase the cooking time of the meat until your appropriate tenderness has been achieved.

CLASSICAL
Fried Chicken

🥣 Prep Time: 15 mins
🕒 Total Time: 1 hr 30 mins

Servings per Recipe: 8
Calories   607 kcal
Fat   40.4 g
Carbohydrates   13.4g
Protein   45.1 g
Cholesterol   174 mg
Sodium   821 mg

Ingredients

1 clove crushed garlic
1/4 lb. butter, melted
1 C. dried bread crumbs
1/3 C. grated Parmesan cheese
2 tbsp chopped fresh parsley

1 tsp salt
1/8 tsp ground black pepper
1 (4 lb.) chicken, cut into pieces

Directions

1. Set your oven to 350 degrees F before doing anything else and grease a 13x9-inch baking dish.
2. In a shallow dish, mix together the melted butter and garlic.
3. In another shallow dish, mix together the cheese, breadcrumbs, parsley, salt and black pepper.
4. Coat the chicken pieces in the butter mixture and in the cheese mixture evenly.
5. Arrange the chicken pieces into the prepared baking dish in a single layer.
6. Drizzle with the remaining butter mixture evenly and cook everything in the oven for about 1-1 1/4 hours.

Crispy Paprika Fried Chicken

Prep Time: 30 mins
Total Time: 50 mins

Servings per Recipe: 8
Calories   489 kcal
Fat   21.8 g
Carbohydrates   29.5g
Protein   40.7 g
Cholesterol   116 mg
Sodium   140 mg

Ingredients

1 (4 lb.) chicken, cut into pieces
1 C. buttermilk
2 C. all-purpose flour for coating
1 tsp paprika
salt and pepper to taste
2 quarts vegetable oil for frying

Directions

1. In a shallow dish, place the buttermilk.
2. In another shallow dish, place the flour, salt, black pepper and paprika.
3. Dip the chicken pieces in the buttermilk completely and coat them in the flour mixture.
4. Arrange the chicken pieces on a baking dish and cover with wax paper and keep aside till flour becomes pasty.
5. In a large cast iron skillet, heat the vegetable oil and fry the chicken pieces till browned.
6. Reduce the heat and cook, covered for about 30 minutes.
7. Uncover and increase the heat and cook till crispy.
8. Transfer the chicken pieces onto paper towel lined plates to drain.

BREAKFAST TACOS
From Mexico

Prep Time: 5 mins
Total Time: 15 mins

Servings per Recipe: 4
Calories   537 kcal
Carbohydrates   27.7 g
Cholesterol   343 mg
Fat   34.1 g
Fiber   3.9 g
Protein   30.6 g
Sodium   1298 mg

Ingredients

6 oz. beef sausage
8 (6 inch) corn tortillas
6 eggs
1/4 cup milk
1/2 tsp pepper
1/2 tsp salt
1 cup shredded Monterey Jack cheese
1 dash hot pepper sauce (e.g. Tabasco™), or to taste
1/2 cup salsa

Directions

1. Cook crumbled sausage in a pan at medium heat until golden brown in color.
2. Heat up two different pans at high heat and medium heat.
3. Whisk together eggs, pepper and salt in a bowl, and pour these eggs into the pan at medium heat.
4. Cook until you see that the eggs are firm and continue cooking after adding sausage.
5. Warm up some tortillas in the pan which is at high heat for about 45 seconds each side and add some cheese before filling with the egg and tortilla mixture you have prepared.
6. Also add some hot pepper sauce and salsa according to your taste before serving it.
7. Enjoy.

Ground Turkey Tacos

🥣 Prep Time: 10 mins
🕐 Total Time: 30 mins

Servings per Recipe: 8
Calories	549 kcal
Carbohydrates	39.1 g
Cholesterol	84 mg
Fat	33.8 g
Fiber	8.3 g
Protein	26.7 g
Sodium	872 mg

Ingredients

Tacos:
- 1 tbsp vegetable oil
- 1 pound lean (at least 93%) ground turkey
- 1 (1 oz.) package taco seasoning mix
- 2/3 cup water
- 1 (4.6 oz.) package taco shells

Toppings:
- 2 medium avocados, pitted, peeled and sliced
- 1 cup sliced pineapple (fresh or canned)

Directions

1. Cook turkey in hot oil over medium heat in a large skillet until you see that it is no longer pink.
2. Drain any water and add taco seasoning mix and some water before turning the heat down and cooking it for another 10 minutes or until you find that the sauce is getting thick.
3. Put this into taco shells.

BALSAMIC, DIJON, and Raisin Brown Rice Salad

Prep Time: 15 mins
Total Time: 1 hr

Servings per Recipe: 6
Calories 451 kcal
Fat 23.5 g
Carbohydrates 54.6 g
Protein 7.1 g
Cholesterol 9 mg
Sodium 338 mg

Ingredients

1 1/2 C. uncooked brown rice
3 C. water
1 red bell pepper, thinly sliced
1 C. frozen green peas, thawed
1/2 C. raisins
1/4 sweet onion (such as Vidalia(R)), chopped
1/4 C. chopped Kalamata olives
1/2 C. vegetable oil
1/4 C. balsamic vinegar
1 1/4 tsps Dijon mustard
salt and ground black pepper to taste
1/4 C. feta cheese

Directions

1. Get your water and rice boiling, place a lid on the pot, set the heat to low, and let the contents cook, with a low heat, for 47 mins.
2. Get a bowl, mix: olives, bell pepper, onions, raisins, and peas.
3. Get a 2nd bowl, combine: mustard, vinegar, and veggie oil.
4. Combine both bowls then add in your ice and add some pepper and salt before adding in some cheese.
5. Enjoy.

Creamy Mushrooms with Shrimp Brown Rice

🥣 Prep Time: 20 mins
🕐 Total Time: 35 mins

Servings per Recipe: 6
Calories   317 kcal
Fat   6.3 g
Carbohydrates   43g
Protein   23.8 g
Cholesterol   173 mg
Sodium   1136 mg

Ingredients

2 C. instant brown rice
1 3/4 C. water
6 tbsps soy sauce
6 tbsps water
1/4 C. honey
2 tbsps cider vinegar
2 tbsps cornstarch
2 tbsps olive oil
2 cloves garlic, chopped
2 C. broccoli florets
1 C. baby carrots
1 small white onion, chopped
1/2 tsp black pepper
1 C. sliced fresh mushrooms
1 1/2 lbs uncooked medium shrimp, peeled and deveined

Directions

1. Get a bowl, mix: cornstarch, soy sauce, vinegar, honey, and water.
2. For 8 mins, in the microwave, cook your rice in 1 3/4 C. of water. Then stir it.
3. Stir fry your garlic in olive for 1 min then add in: black pepper, broccoli, onions, and carrots.
4. Continue frying for 7 more mins.
5. Then add the mushrooms and cook for 4 more mins.
6. Empty the pan.
7. Add in your cornstarch mix to the pan and cook it for 1.5 mins then add in your shrimp. Cook the shrimp for 4 mins before pouring in the veggies with the shrimp and reheating everything.
8. Serve the rice with the veggies and shrimp.
9. Enjoy.

EASY AMERICAN
Cheese Burritos

🍲 Prep Time: 15 mins

🕐 Total Time: 1 hr

Servings per Recipe: 1
Calories 400 kcal
Fat 10 g
Carbohydrates 49.9 g
Protein 15.8 g
Cholesterol 29 mg
Sodium 1075 mg

Ingredients

1 (10 inch) flour tortilla
1/4 C. vegetarian refried beans
1 slice American cheese
1 pinch ground black pepper
1 tsp low-fat sour cream

1 dash hot pepper sauce

Directions

1. For five mins warm your refried beans.
2. Then warm your tortillas in the microwave for 30 secs.
3. Layer beans into the tortilla then some sour cream then cheese, and some pepper.
4. Finally add some hot sauce.
5. Form everything into a burrito.

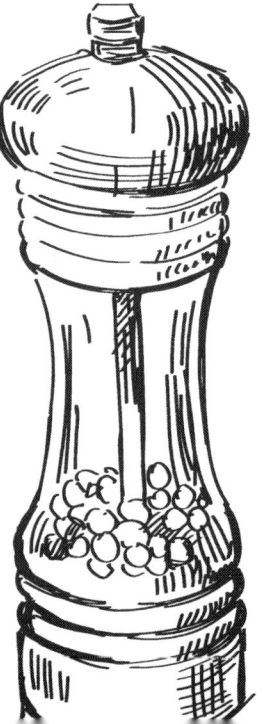

Cabbage and Cheddar Burritos

🥣 Prep Time: 20 mins
🕐 Total Time: 45 mins

Servings per Recipe: 8
Calories 448 kcal
Fat 19.3 g
Carbohydrates 44.3g
Protein 24 g
Cholesterol 58 mg
Sodium 647 mg

Ingredients

1 1/2 lbs ground round
1/2 medium head cabbage, chopped
1 1/2 onion, chopped
1 tbsp minced garlic
1 tsp crushed red pepper flakes
1 tsp ground black pepper

1 C. water
8 (10 inch) flour tortillas
2 C. shredded Cheddar cheese

Directions

1. Fry your beef in hot oil. Once is it is fully cooked crumble it. Remove any oil excesses from the pan then add in the following: water, cabbage, black pepper, onion, red pepper flakes, and garlic.
2. Stir fry for 11 min until all water is gone.
3. Warm the tortillas in another pan for a few secs.
4. With a spoon fill each tortilla with some meat. Than top the meat with one fourth a C. of cheddar.
5. Roll into a burrito.
6. Continue for all remaining tortillas and meat.
7. Enjoy.

SQUASH AND TOMATOES
Burritos

🥣 Prep Time: 15 mins
🕐 Total Time: 25 mins

Servings per Recipe: 2
Calories   478 kcal
Fat   24.1 g
Carbohydrates   49.7g
Protein   17.6 g
Cholesterol   36 mg
Sodium   865 mg

Ingredients

1 tbsp olive oil
1/2 onion, chopped
3 small summer squash, sliced
salt to taste
4 (7 inch) flour tortillas
1/2 C. shredded Cheddar cheese
1/2 C. chopped tomato

Directions

1. Fry your onion in olive oil for 4 mins. Then mix in one third of your squash let it get soft.
2. Then add another third. Let it get soft. Then add the last of it.
3. Add some salt for seasoning.
4. For 10 sec microwave your tortillas.
5. Then fill each one with some spoonfuls of squash.
6. Then layer some tomatoes and cheddar. Form a burrito and enjoy.

Classical Empanada I

Prep Time: 15 mins
Total Time: 40 mins

Servings per Recipe: 12
Calories	226 kcal
Carbohydrates	32.1 g
Cholesterol	28 mg
Fat	10.3 g
Fiber	0.7 g
Protein	1.8 g
Sodium	84 mg

Ingredients

1/2 cup butter, softened
1 (3 ounce) package cream cheese
1 cup sifted all-purpose flour
1 cup fruit preserves
1/3 cup white sugar
1 tsp ground cinnamon

Directions

1. Whisk butter, flour and cream together until smooth before shaping it up and wrapping it in foil to be placed in the refrigerator for at least one night.
2. Set your oven to 375 degrees F.
3. Roll the dough on a floured surface before cutting it with a cookie cutter and placing jam in the center of each one.
4. Bake this in the preheated oven for about 20 minutes before coating it with the mixture of cinnamon and sugar.

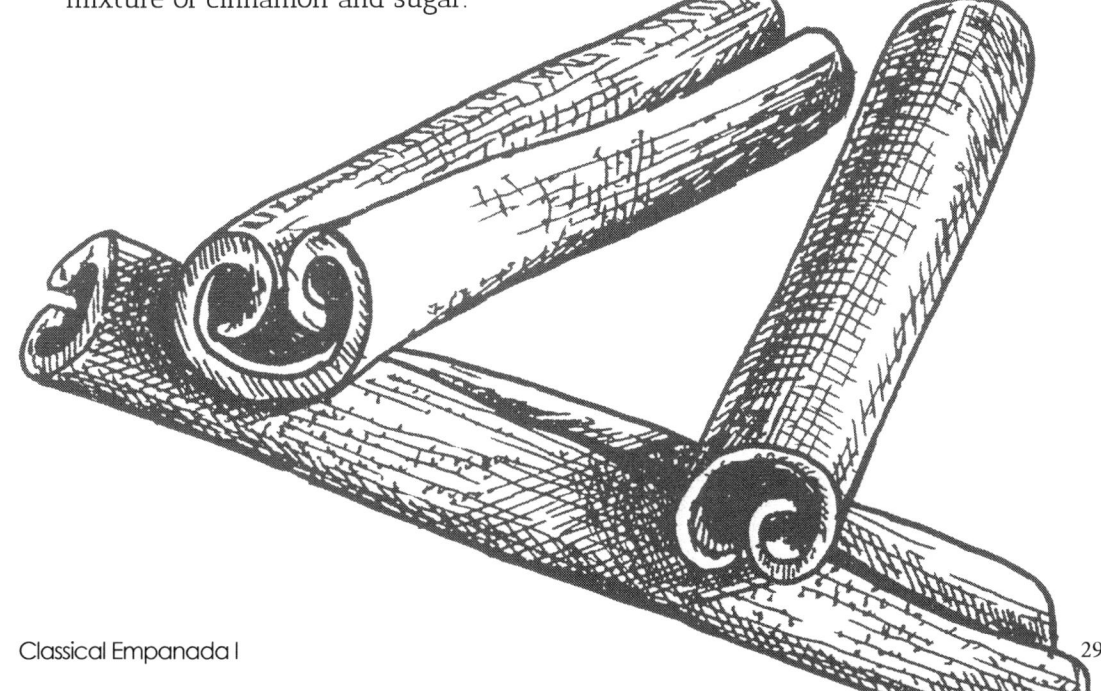

FRIED
Empanada

🥣 Prep Time: 20 mins
🕐 Total Time: 2hrs 20 mins

Servings per Recipe: 12
Calories   798 kcal
Carbohydrates   27.4 g
Cholesterol   76 mg
Fat   63.9 g
Fiber   2.1 g
Protein   31 g
Sodium   1754 mg

Ingredients

4 1/2 cups all-purpose flour
1 1/2 tsps salt
1/2 cup shortening
1 1/4 cups water, or as needed
2 tbsps olive oil
1 small onion, chopped
1 1/2 pounds ground beef
1 pinch salt
2 tbsps paprika

1 tbsp cumin
1/2 tsp ground black pepper
1/2 cup raisins
1 tbsp white vinegar
2 hard-cooked eggs, peeled and chopped
1 quart oil for frying, or as needed

Directions

1. Mix salt, flour and sliced shortening very thoroughly before adding water and turning all this into a ball shaped dough to be put into refrigerator wrapped in plastic wrap.
2. Cook onion in hot oil for a few minutes before adding beef, salt, paprika, cumin and black pepper, and cook until beef is brown before adding vinegar and raisins.
3. Cool it down before adding some hard cooked eggs into it.
4. Make 2 inch balls out of dough and after rolling it up on a floured surface; put some meat into it before folding it into half-moon shapes.
5. Deep fry one or two at a time for about 5 minutes
6. Serve.

Valencian Empanadas

 Prep Time: 20 mins
 Total Time: 30 mins

Servings per Recipe: 12
Calories	124 kcal
Carbohydrates	12.6 g
Cholesterol	41 mg
Fat	5.7 g
Fiber	0.7 g
Protein	5.1 g
Sodium	319 mg

Ingredients

2 tbsps olive oil
1 medium onion, chopped
2 small tomatoes - peeled, seeded and chopped
4 ounces diced cooked turkey
2 hard-cooked eggs, chopped
1 1/2 tbsps chopped fresh parsley
salt and pepper to taste
1 (10 ounce) can refrigerated pizza crust dough

Directions

1. Cook onion in hot oil for a few minutes before adding tomatoes and turkey with a difference of one minute.
2. After few minutes of cooking; stir in eggs and some parsley, and let it cool down for at least five minutes.
3. Set your oven to 425 degrees F before rolling the can of pizza and cutting twelve 3 inch squares out of it.
4. Fill this up with the filling and fold it around this filling before baking this for about ten minutes or until golden brown.
5. Let it stand for five minutes before serving.

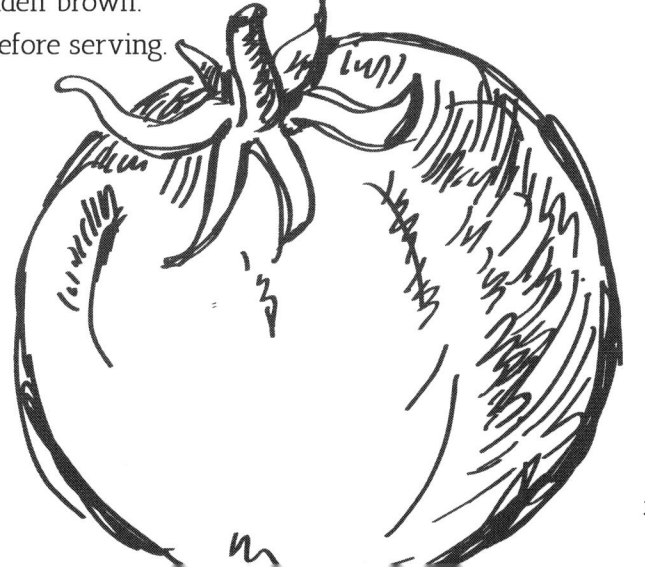

CHIPOTLE
Caesar Bacon Sandwich

Prep Time: 10 mins
Total Time: 15 mins

Servings per Recipe: 1
Calories   1243 kcal
Carbohydrates   31.9 g
Cholesterol   312 mg
Fat   83.9 g
Fiber   1.5 g
Protein   85.7 g
Sodium   1813 mg

Ingredients

2 slices sourdough bread
1/4 C. Caesar salad dressing
1 cooked chicken breast, diced
1/2 C. shredded Cheddar cheese
1 tbsp turkey bacon bits
1 1/2 tsps chipotle chili powder, or to taste
2 tbsps softened butter

Directions

1. Heat up your Panini grill according to the instruction of the manufacturer.
2. Spread Caesar dressing over each half of the bread before putting chicken, cheddar cheese, bacon bits and chipotle chili powder over the lower half, and closing it up to make a sandwich.
3. Put some butter on top and cook this Panini in the preheated grill for about 4 minutes or until the outside is golden brown.

Romano, Basil, Chicken Sandwich

🥣 Prep Time: 20 mins
🕐 Total Time: 36 mins

Servings per Recipe: 2
Calories   587 kcal
Carbohydrates   20 g
Cholesterol   85 mg
Fat   41.5 g
Fiber   1.8 g
Protein   32.5 g
Sodium   523 mg

Ingredients

- 1/4 C. packed fresh basil leaves
- 1/4 C. olive oil
- 4 cloves garlic, diced
- 2 tbsps grated Romano cheese
- 1 tsp dried oregano
- 1 tsp ground black pepper
- 2 skinless, boneless chicken breast halves
- 2 tbsps creamy Caesar salad dressing
- 6 slices Italian bread with sesame seeds (Scali)
- 1/2 C. shredded iceberg lettuce
- 2 thin slices smoked mozzarella

Directions

1. Heat up your grill and put some oil on the grate
2. Blend a mixture of basil, oregano, oil, garlic, Romano cheese and pepper in a blender until smooth.
3. Now grill chicken on the preheated grill for about 5 minutes each side.
4. Spread Caesar dressing over the bread and put lettuce before putting additional slice of bread over it.
5. Now put cooked chicken breast and smoked mozzarella before closing it up to make a sandwich.
6. Cook this Panini in the preheated grill for about three minutes or until the outside is golden brown.

SOURDOUGH, Provolone, Pesto Sandwich

🥣 Prep Time: 15 mins
🕒 Total Time: 19 mins

Servings per Recipe: 4
Calories   1243 kcal
Carbohydrates   31.9 g
Cholesterol   312 mg
Fat   83.9 g
Fiber   1.5 g
Protein   85.7 g
Sodium   1813 mg

Ingredients

1/2 C. Extra Virgin Olive Oil
8 slices sourdough bread
1/4 C. pesto
16 thin slices Provolone cheese
12 thin slices turkey

4 whole, roasted red peppers, julienned

Directions

1. Heat up your Panini grill according to the instruction of the manufacturer.
2. Spread pesto over each half of the bread before putting ½ of cheese, turkey, pepper strips and the remaining cheese over the lower half, and closing it up to make a sandwich.
3. Put some butter on top and cook this Panini in the preheated grill for about 4 minutes or until the outside is golden brown.

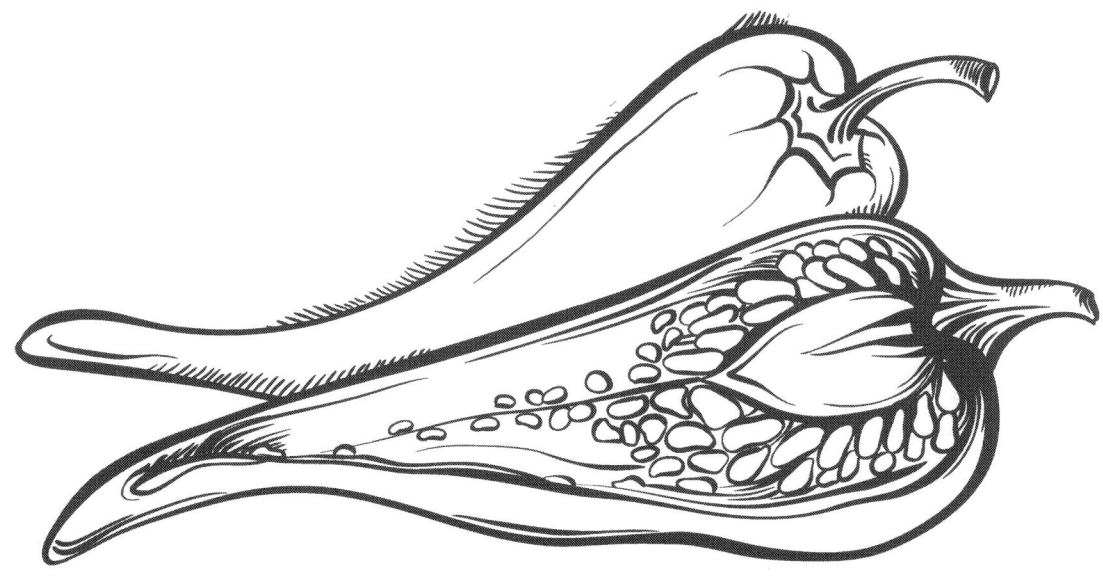

Avocado, Turkey, Spinach, Ciabatta

Prep Time: 10 mins
Total Time: 20 mins

Servings per Recipe: 2
Calories	469 kcal
Carbohydrates	45.5 g
Cholesterol	37 mg
Fat	23.8 g
Fiber	8.5 g
Protein	22.1 g
Sodium	1250 mg

Ingredients

- 4 slices artisan bread such as ciabatta
- 2 tsps honey Dijon salad dressing
- 1/2 C. baby spinach leaves
- 1/4 lb sliced oven-roasted deli turkey breast
- 1/4 red onion, cut into strips
- 1 ripe avocado from Mexico, peeled, pitted and thickly sliced
- Salt and pepper to taste
- 1/4 C. crumbled soft goat cheese
- Non-stick cooking spray

Directions

1. Heat up your Panini grill according to the instruction of the manufacturer.
2. Spread honey Dijon dressing, spinach leaves, turkey breast and red onion over lower half of the bread before putting avocado slices, salt, pepper and goat cheese over the upper half, and closing it up to make a sandwich.
3. Put some butter on top and cook this Panini in the preheated grill for about 8 minutes or until the outside is golden brown.

SESAME RAMEN
Coleslaw

🥣 Prep Time: 15 mins
🕐 Total Time: 25 mins

Servings per Recipe: 4
Calories	253 kcal
Carbohydrates	30.5 g
Cholesterol	0 mg
Fat	12.5 g
Fiber	5.1 g
Protein	7.1 g
Sodium	543 mg

Ingredients

- 2 tbsps vegetable oil
- 3 tbsps white vinegar
- 2 tbsps white sugar
- 1 (3 ounce) package chicken flavored ramen noodles, crushed, seasoning packet reserved
- 1/2 tsp salt
- 1/2 tsp ground black pepper
- 2 tbsps sesame seeds
- 1/4 cup sliced almonds
- 1/2 medium head cabbage, shredded
- 5 green onions, chopped

Directions

1. Set your oven at 350 degrees F and also put some oil on the baking dish.
2. Mix oil, ramen noodle mix, salt, vinegar, pepper and sugar in a bowl to be used as a dressing.
3. Bake sesame seeds and almonds in the preheated oven for about 10 minutes.
4. Coat the mixture of cabbage, crushed ramen noodles and greens onions with the dressing very thoroughly before topping it with sesame seeds and almonds.
5. Serve.

Broccoli Ramen Salad

🥣 Prep Time: 15 mins
🕐 Total Time: 1 hr

Servings per Recipe: 6
Calories   280 kcal
Carbohydrates   53.6 g
Cholesterol   0 mg
Fat   4.4 g
Fiber   1.3 g
Protein   10.4 g
Sodium   1351 mg

Ingredients

1 (16 ounce) package broccoli coleslaw mix
2 (3 ounce) packages chicken flavored ramen noodles
1 bunch green onions, chopped
1 cup unsalted peanuts
1 cup sunflower seeds

1/2 cup white sugar
1/4 cup vegetable oil
1/3 cup cider vinegar

Directions

1. Coat a mixture of green onions, slaw and broken noodles with the mixture of sugar, ramen seasoning packets, oil and vinegar very thoroughly before refrigerating it for at least one hour.
2. Garnish with peanuts and sunflower seeds before serving it.

VENETIAN BEEF
Ramen Stir-Fry

🥣 Prep Time: 10 mins
🕒 Total Time: 45 mins

Servings per Recipe: 6
Calories   297 kcal
Carbohydrates   7.4 g
Cholesterol   78 mg
Fat   18.4 g
Fiber   1.2 g
Protein   23.6 g
Sodium   546 mg

Ingredients

1 pound ground beef, or to taste
16 slices pepperoni, or to taste
1 (14.5 ounce) can diced tomatoes
1 cup water
2 (3 ounce) packages beef-flavored ramen noodles
1 green bell peppers, cut into strips
1 cup shredded mozzarella cheese

Directions

1. Cook beef and pepperoni slices over high heat in a large skillet for about 7 minutes before adding tomatoes, content of seasoning packet content from ramen noodles and water into skillet containing beef.
2. After breaking ramen noodles into half, add this to the beef mixture along with green bell pepper and cook all this for about five minutes or until you see that noodles are soft.
3. Turn the heat off before adding mozzarella cheese and letting it melt down before serving.

Natural Ramen Noodles

Prep Time: 10 mins
Total Time: 20 mins

Servings per Recipe: 4
Calories	280 kcal
Carbohydrates	53.6 g
Cholesterol	0 mg
Fat	4.4 g
Fiber	1.3 g
Protein	10.4 g
Sodium	1351 mg

Ingredients

- 4 cups vegetable broth
- 4 cups water
- 1 tbsp soy sauce
- 1 tbsp sesame oil
- 1 tbsp ground ginger
- 1 tbsp Sriracha hot sauce
- 9 ounces soba noodles

Directions

1. Bring everything except noodles to boil before adding noodles and cooking it for about seven minutes or until you see that they are tender.
2. Take noodles out into bowls and top with broth according to your choice.

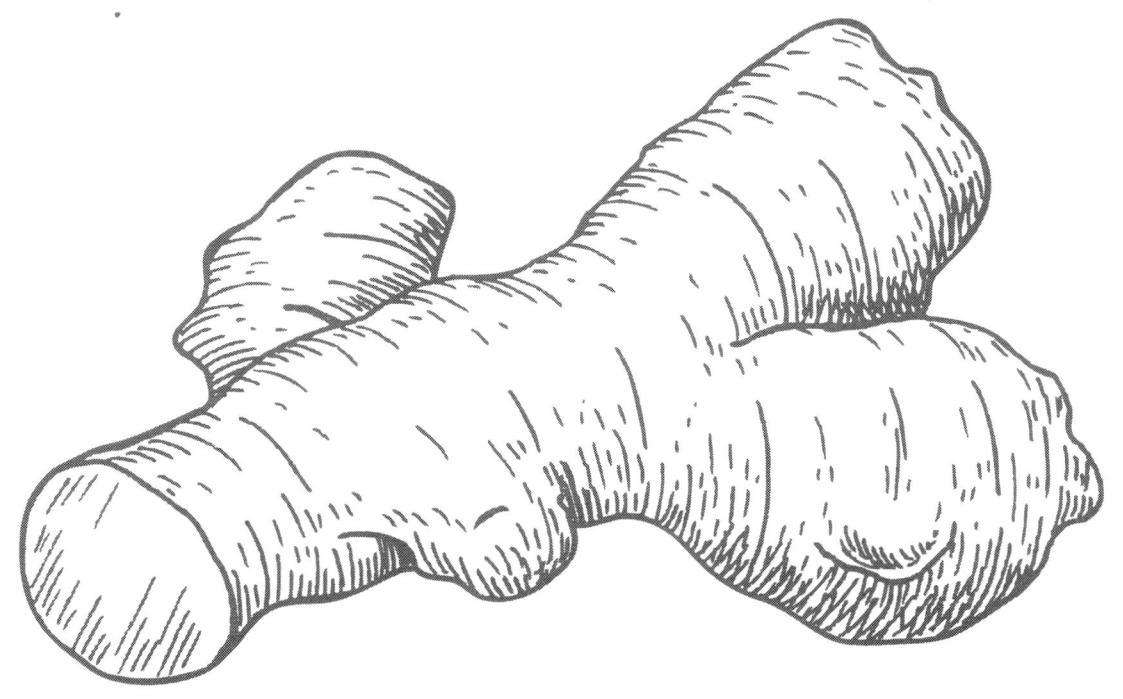

CABBAGE RAMEN
Salad I

🍲 Prep Time: 15 mins
🕐 Total Time: 25 mins

Servings per Recipe: 6
Calories   266 kcal
Carbohydrates   16.2 g
Cholesterol   < 1 mg
Fat   22.6 g
Fiber   3.2 g
Protein   1.8 g
Sodium   82 mg

Ingredients

1/2 large head cabbage, coarsely chopped
1 (3 ounce) package ramen noodles, crushed
1/2 cup sunflower seeds
1/2 cup vegetable oil
3 tbsps white sugar
3 tbsps distilled white vinegar

Directions

1. Pour a mixture of vinegar, ramen flavor packet, sugar and oil over the mixture of cabbage, sunflower seeds and noodles.
2. Mix it very thoroughly before serving.

Ramen for College

Prep Time: 5 mins
Total Time: 15 mins

Servings per Recipe: 1
Calories	500 kcal
Carbohydrates	66 g
Cholesterol	191 mg
Fat	19.2 g
Fiber	4.5 g
Protein	17.4 g
Sodium	1796 mg

Ingredients

2 1/2 cups water
1 carrot, sliced
4 fresh mushrooms, sliced
1 (3 ounce) package ramen noodle pasta with flavor packet

1 egg, lightly beaten
1/4 cup milk (optional)

Directions

1. Cook carrots and mushrooms in boiling water for about seven minutes before adding noodles and flavoring packets, and cooking all this for three more minutes.
2. Pour egg into the mixture very slowly, while stirring continuously for thirty seconds to get the egg cooked.
3. Add some milk before serving.

EASY RAMEN
Soup

🍲 Prep Time: 5 mins
🕐 Total Time: 15 mins

Servings per Recipe: 2
Calories   291 kcal
Carbohydrates   42.4 g
Cholesterol   0 mg
Fat   10.2 g
Fiber   2.2 g
Protein   6.9 g
Sodium   1675 mg

Ingredients

3 1/2 cups vegetable broth
1 (3.5 ounce) package ramen noodles with dried vegetables
2 tsps soy sauce
1/2 tsp chili oil
1/2 tsp minced fresh ginger root

2 green onions, sliced

Directions

1. Bring a mixture of noodles and broth to boil over high heat before turning down the heat to medium and adding soy sauce, ginger and chili oil.
2. Cook this for about 10 minutes before adding sesame oil.
3. Garnish this with green onions before serving.

Cheesy Ramen

Prep Time: 5 mins
Total Time: 5 mins

Servings per Recipe: 1
Calories	163 kcal
Carbohydrates	7.9 g
Cholesterol	27 mg
Fat	11.3 g
Fiber	0.4 g
Protein	7.5 g
Sodium	733 mg

Ingredients

2 cups water
1 (3 ounce) package any flavor ramen noodles
1 slice American cheese

Directions

1. Cook ramen noodles in boiling water for about 2 minutes and drain it with the help of colander before stirring in seasoning packet and cheese.
2. Serve.

CABBAGE RAMEN
Salad II

🍜 Prep Time: 30 mins
🕐 Total Time: 30 mins

Servings per Recipe: 12
Calories   384 kcal
Carbohydrates   26.6 g
Cholesterol   0 mg
Fat   29.7 g
Fiber   3.7 g
Protein   5.7 g
Sodium   290 mg

Ingredients

1 1/4 pounds red cabbage, chopped
2 (3 ounce) packages ramen noodles, broken into small pieces
1 cup chopped red bell pepper
1 cup chopped green onion
3/4 cup slivered almonds
1/2 cup roasted sunflower seeds
1/2 cup toasted sesame seeds
1/2 cup white sugar

1/2 cup peanut oil
1/2 cup olive oil
1/4 cup red vinegar
1/2 tsp ground black pepper

Directions

1. Combine all the ingredients mentioned above very thoroughly in a large re-sealable bag very thoroughly before serving it to anyone.

Jalapeno Lime Sirloin Taco

🥣 Prep Time: 15 mins
🕐 Total Time: 45 mins

Servings per Recipe: 9	
Calories	379 kcal
Fat	21.4 g
Carbohydrates	28.1g
Protein	20.3 g
Cholesterol	58 mg
Sodium	69 mg

Ingredients

- 2 lbs top sirloin steak, cut into thin strips
- salt and ground black pepper to taste
- 1/4 C. vegetable oil
- 18 (6 inch) corn tortillas
- 1 onion, diced
- 4 fresh jalapeno peppers, seeded and chopped
- 1 bunch fresh cilantro, chopped
- 4 limes, cut into wedges

Directions

1. Stir fry your steak for 6 mins. Then coat it with some pepper and salt. Set it aside.
2. Add more oil to the pan and fry your tortillas.
3. Layer cilantro, steak, jalapenos, and onions on each fried tortilla and then garnish with some lime.
4. Enjoy.

SWISS CHARD and Onions Taco

🍲 Prep Time: 20 mins
🕐 Total Time: 1 hr 5 mins

Servings per Recipe: 4
Calories 354 kcal
Fat 13 g
Carbohydrates 48.8g
Protein 14.4 g
Cholesterol 20 mg
Sodium 531 mg

Ingredients

1 1/2 tbsps olive oil
1 large onion, cut into 1/4-inch slices
3 cloves garlic, minced
1 tbsp red pepper flakes, or to taste
1/2 C. chicken broth
1 bunch Swiss chard, tough stems removed and leaves cut crosswise into 1 1/2-inch slices

1 pinch salt
12 corn tortillas
1 C. crumbled queso fresco cheese
3/4 C. salsa

Directions

1. Stir fry your onions for 11 mins and then combine in some red pepper flakes, and garlic and cook for another 2 mins.
2. Add into the onions: salt, chicken broth, and Swiss chard.
3. Place a lid on the pan and set the heat to low. Simmer for 7 mins.
4. Take off the lid and raise the heat a bit. Stir the contents for 6 mins until no liquid remains.
5. Shut off the heat fully.
6. Get a 2nd pan and toast the tortillas for 2 mins each side with a low level of heat.
7. Layer queso fresco cheese, chard mix, and salsa on each tortilla.
8. Enjoy.

Guacamole and Tomatoes Taco

🥣 Prep Time: 15 mins
🕐 Total Time: 20 mins

Servings per Recipe: 6
Calories	455 kcal
Fat	21.1 g
Carbohydrates	70.1g
Protein	13.8 g
Cholesterol	0 mg
Sodium	604 mg

Ingredients

- 1 (14.5 oz.) can whole tomatoes, drained, rinsed, patted dry
- 2 roma tomatoes, quartered
- 1 onion, chopped, divided
- 1 clove garlic, coarsely chopped
- 1/4 C. fresh cilantro
- 1/2 jalapeno pepper
- salt and pepper to taste
- 4 avocados, halved with pits removed
- 12 (6 inch) whole wheat tortillas
- 1 (15 oz.) can kidney beans, rinsed and drained
- 2 C. torn romaine lettuce

Directions

1. Set your oven to 350 degrees before doing anything else.
2. Enter the following into a blender or processor: jalapenos, fresh and canned tomatoes, garlic, and half of your onions.
3. Process or pulse a few times. Do not make a smooth mix. Only dice the contents a bit.
4. Get a bowl, mix until smooth: pepper, the rest of the onions, salt, and avocados.
5. Get a casserole dish and cook your tortillas in the oven for 5 mins.
6. Layer on each tortilla: lettuce, guacamole, salsa, and beans.
7. Enjoy.

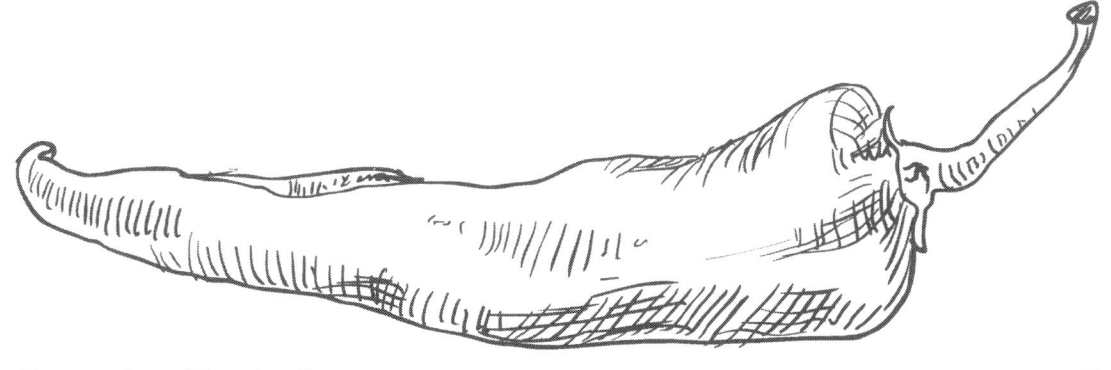

COLESLAW
Taco

🥣 Prep Time: 20 mins
🕒 Total Time: 20 mins

Servings per Recipe: 6
Calories   27 kcal
Fat   0.1 g
Carbohydrates   6.6g
Protein   1.1 g
Cholesterol   0 mg
Sodium   19 mg

Ingredients

1/2 small head cabbage, chopped
1 jalapeno pepper, seeded and minced
1/2 red onion, minced
1 carrot, chopped

1 tbsp chopped fresh cilantro
1 lime, juiced

Directions

1. Simply combine all the ingredients in a bowl.
2. Enjoy on warm tortillas with your choice of meat and salsa.

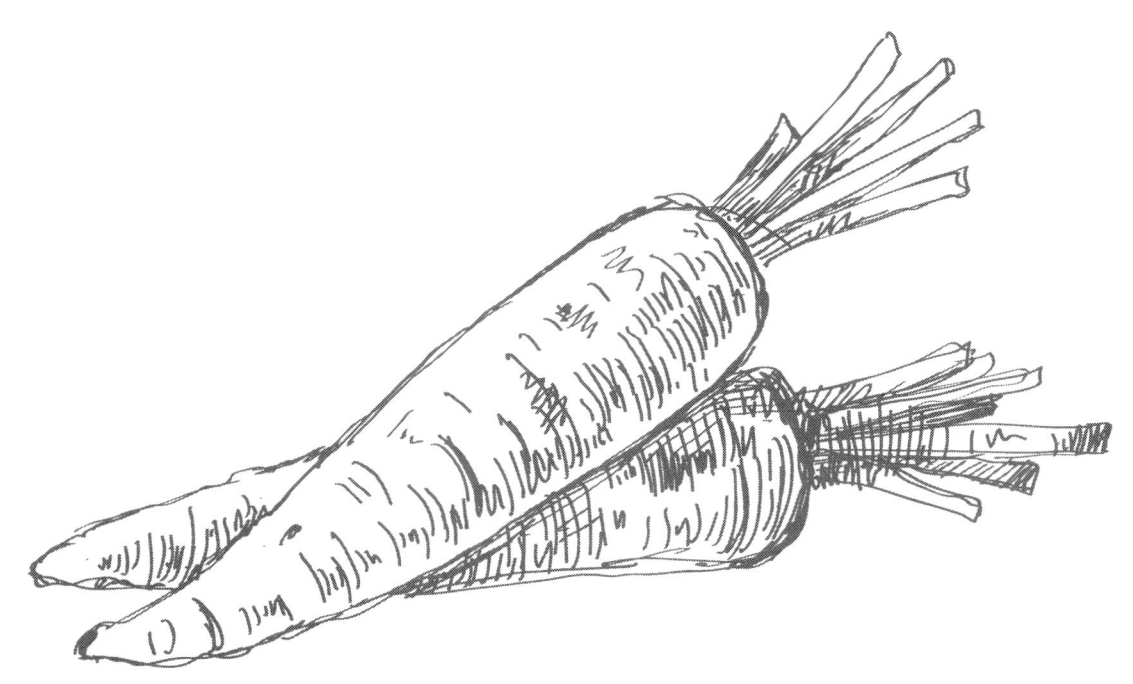

Corn and Beef Taco

Prep Time: 15 mins
Total Time: 45 mins

Servings per Recipe: 8
Calories	520 kcal
Fat	30.7 g
Carbohydrates	32.6 g
Protein	26.7 g
Cholesterol	96 mg
Sodium	1289 mg

Ingredients

- 2 lbs ground beef
- 1 onion, chopped
- 2 (15 oz.) cans ranch-style beans
- 1 (15.25 oz.) can whole kernel corn
- 1 (10 oz.) can diced tomatoes with green chile peppers
- 1 (14.5 oz.) can peeled and diced tomatoes with juice
- 1 (1.25 oz.) package taco seasoning mix

Directions

1. Cook your onions and beef for 10 mins then remove oil excesses.
2. Combine with the beef your chili peppers, beans, taco seasoning, tomatoes, and corn. Stir the contents for a min. Cook over medium heat for 17 mins.
3. Enjoy.

SHRIMP and Cilantro Taco

🥣 Prep Time: 15 mins
🕐 Total Time: 47 mins

Servings per Recipe: 4
Calories   567 kcal
Fat   23.1 g
Carbohydrates   59.5g
Protein   31.2 g
Cholesterol   188 mg
Sodium   951 mg

Ingredients

1 mango - peeled, seeded and diced
1 ripe avocado - peeled, pitted, and diced
2 tomatoes, diced
1/2 C. chopped fresh cilantro
1/4 C. chopped red onion
3 cloves garlic, minced

1/2 tsp salt
2 tbsps lime juice
1/4 C. honey butter
1 lb salad shrimp
4 (10 inch) flour tortillas, warmed

Directions

1. Get bowl combine: lime juice, mango, salt, avocadoes, garlic, onions, and cilantro. Place a lid or some plastic wrap on the bowl.
2. Put the bowl in the fridge for 40 mins.
3. Stir fry your shrimp for 4 mins in the honey butter.
4. Layer on your tortillas: mango mix, and shrimp.
5. Enjoy.

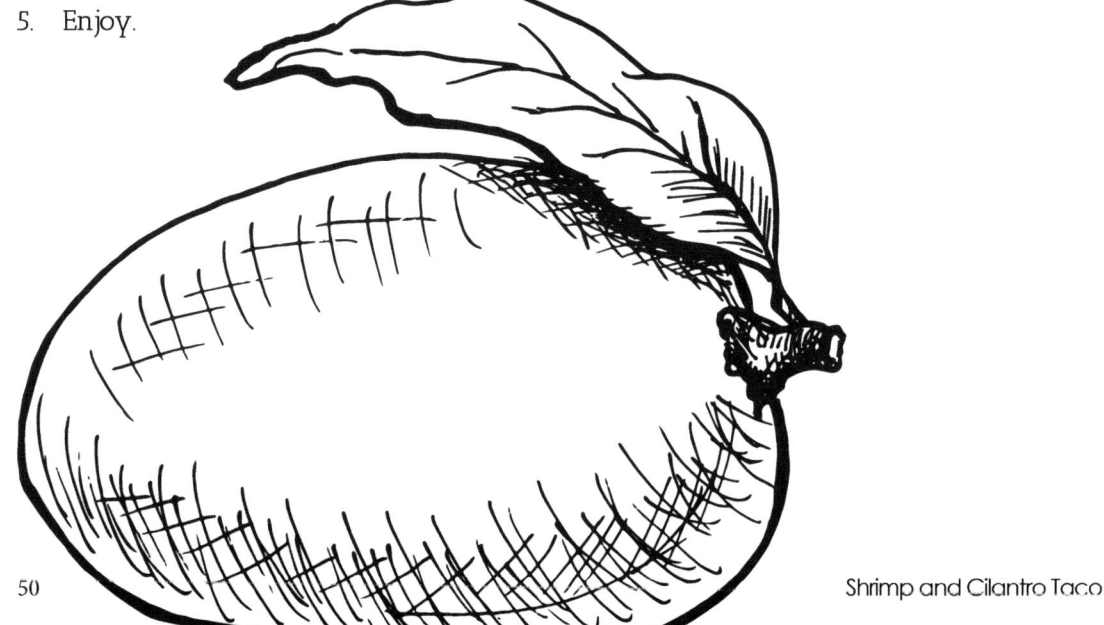

Teriyaki Steak Tacos

🥣 Prep Time: 30 mins
🕐 Total Time: 40 mins

Servings per Recipe: 2
Calories	465 kcal
Fat	15 g
Carbohydrates	69.7g
Protein	33.2 g
Cholesterol	49 mg
Sodium	3853 mg

Ingredients

- 4 Mission(R) Soft Taco Flour Tortillas
- 8 oz. sirloin steak, chopped into 1x1/4-inch pieces
- 1/2 C. teriyaki marinade
- 1/2 C. cucumber, grated
- 1/2 C. carrots, shredded
- 1/2 tsp fresh ginger, grated
- 1/2 tsp black sesame seeds
- 1 tbsp fresh orange juice
- 1/2 tsp soy sauce
- 1/2 tsp honey
- Salt and pepper to taste
- 1/2 C. sliced green onions

Directions

1. Get a bowl, mix: teriyaki and steak.
2. Place a lid on the container and put it in the fridge for 30 mins.
3. Get a 2nd bowl, combine: honey, pepper, cucumbers, ginger, soy sauce, carrots, sesame seeds, salt, and orange juice.
4. Put this in the fridge as well with a covering until you are ready to assemble your tacos.
5. Stir fry your steak and marinade for 12 mins.
6. Layer the following on each tortillas: sliced green onions, one fourth C. of carrot mix, and an even amount of steak.

CHEDDAR BEEF
Taco

🥣 Prep Time: 15 mins
🕐 Total Time: 2hrs 20 mins

Servings per Recipe: 16
Calories 338 kcal
Fat 16.1 g
Carbohydrates 32.7g
Protein 14.8 g
Cholesterol 42 mg
Sodium 708 mg

Ingredients

10 fluid oz. warm water
3/4 tsp salt
3 tbsps vegetable oil
4 C. all-purpose flour
2 tsps active dry yeast
1 (6 oz.) can tomato paste
3/4 C. water
1 (1.25 oz.) package taco seasoning mix, divided
1 tsp chili powder, or to taste
1/2 tsp cayenne pepper, or to taste
1 (16 oz.) can fat-free refried beans
1/3 C. salsa
1/4 C. chopped onion
1/2 lb ground beef
4 C. shredded Cheddar cheese

Directions

1. Enter the following into a bread machine: yeast, water, flour, oil, and salt.
2. Use the dough cycle.
3. Occasionally check the dough to make sure it is not too dry if so add some water.
4. Get a bowl, mix: 3/4 taco seasoning, cayenne pepper, water chili powder, and tomato paste.
5. Get a 2nd bowl, mix: onions, salsa, and refried beans.
6. Set your oven to 400 degrees before doing anything else.
7. Stir fry your ground beef remove oil excesses. Then put some water and the rest of the taco seasoning.
8. Let the contents simmer for 4 mins then shut the heat.
9. Take your dough, once the machine is done, and break it into two pieces.
10. Flatten the dough into two 12 inch circular layers.
11. On each dough piece layer: tomato mix, bean mix, beef, and cheese.
12. Cook in the oven for 17 mins.
13. After 7 mins turn the contents.

Beans and White Rice Taco

🥣 Prep Time: 15 mins
🕐 Total Time: 45 mins

Servings per Recipe: 4
Calories   512 kcal
Fat   23.7 g
Carbohydrates   67.2g
Protein   13.7 g
Cholesterol   0 mg
Sodium   448 mg

Ingredients

3 tomatoes, seeded and chopped
2 avocados, chopped
1 small onion, chopped
1/4 C. chopped fresh cilantro
2 cloves garlic, minced
1 lime, juiced
2 tbsps vegetable oil
8 corn tortillas

1 (15 oz.) can black beans, drained and rinsed
1 C. cooked white rice
2 tbsps chopped fresh cilantro
1 dash green pepper sauce

Directions

1. Get a bowl, combine then toss: garlic, tomatoes, lime juice, one fourth C. cilantro, onions, and avocados.
2. For 2 mins per side cook your tortillas in veggie oil.
3. Layer on each tortilla: 2 tbsps of beans, tomato mix, 2 tbsps of cilantro and green pepper sauce, 2 tbsps of cooked rice.
4. Enjoy.

TEMPEH and Veggie Broth Vegetarian Tacos

🍲 Prep Time: 15 mins
🕒 Total Time: 30 mins

Servings per Recipe: 4
Calories   199 kcal
Fat   13 g
Carbohydrates   11.4g
Protein   10.9 g
Cholesterol   0 mg
Sodium   392 m

Ingredients

2 tbsps extra virgin olive oil
1 small onion, minced
2 cloves garlic, minced
1 (8 oz.) package spicy flavored tempeh, coarsely grated
1/2 C. vegetable broth
2 tbsps taco seasoning mix

1 tsp dried oregano
1/2 tsp ground red pepper (optional)

Directions

1. Stir fry your onions for 6 mins in oil. Combine in garlic and cook for another 3 mins. Add in your tempeh and cook for 6 more mins.
2. Add in the veggie broth to the onions, add in the taco seasoning, red pepper, and oregano.
3. Lower the heat and let the mix cook until all the liquid is removed. This should take about 7 mins.
4. Layer the mix on tacos or tortillas.
5. Enjoy.

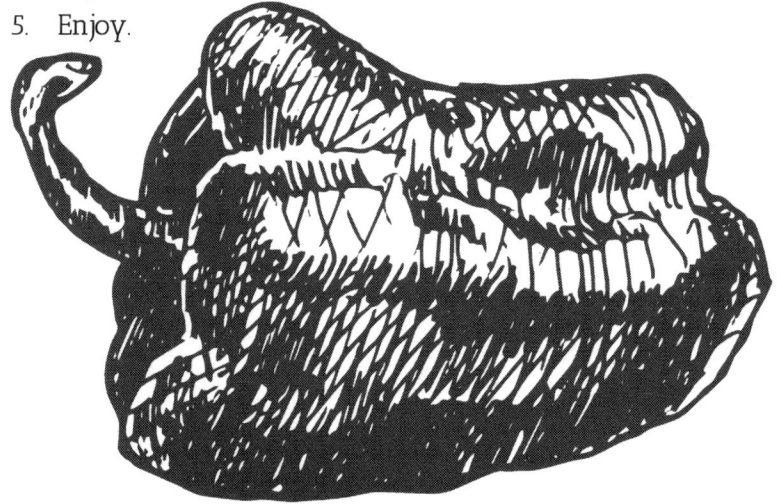

Soft and Hard Shell Tacos

 Prep Time: 10 mins
 Total Time: 30 mins

Servings per Recipe: 10
Calories 347 kcal
Fat 16 g
Carbohydrates 31.9 g
Protein 17.5 g
Cholesterol 49 mg
Sodium 801 mg

Ingredients

1 1/4 lbs ground beef
1/2 onion, chopped
1 (1.25 oz.) package dry taco seasoning mix
3/4 C. water
1 (14 oz.) can refried beans
4 oz. process cheese food (such as Velveeta(R)), cut into small cubes
10 (6 inch) flour tortillas, warmed
10 crisp taco shells, warmed

Directions

1. For 11 mins fry your onions and beef. Then remove any excess oils.
2. Get a saucepan and add water and taco seasoning.
3. Get this mixture boiling.
4. Once boiling lower the heat and let it simmer for 12 mins.
5. After 12 mins combine the taco seasoning mix with the beef and let the contents continue to lightly boil.
6. Get a 2nd saucepan and mix cubed cheese and refried beans together. Heat for 10 mins stir and heat for 12 more mins.
7. Layer each tortilla with an equal amount of refried beans and cheese. Fold each tortilla around a taco.
8. Then add in your seasoned ground beef.

ORIENTAL
Coleslaw

🥣 Prep Time: 15 mins
🕐 Total Time: 25 mins

Servings per Recipe: 4
Calories   253 kcal
Fat   12.5 g
Carbohydrates   30.5g
Protein   7.1 g
Cholesterol   0 mg
Sodium   543 mg

Ingredients

2 tbsp vegetable oil
3 tbsp white vinegar
2 tbsp white sugar
1 (3 oz.) package chicken flavored ramen noodles, crushed, seasoning packet reserved
1/2 tsp salt
1/2 tsp ground black pepper

2 tbsp sesame seeds
1/4 C. sliced almonds
1/2 medium head cabbage, shredded
5 green onions, chopped

Directions

1. Set your oven to 350 degrees F before doing anything else.
2. For dressing in a medium bowl, add the oil, vinegar, sugar, ramen noodle spice mix, salt and pepper and beat till well combined.
3. In a medium baking sheet, place the sesame seeds and almonds in a single layer.
4. Cook in the oven for about 10 minutes.
5. In a large salad bowl, mix together the cabbage, green onions and crushed ramen noodles.
6. Add the dressing and toss to coat well.
7. Serve with a topping of the toasted sesame seeds and almonds.

Garden Party Coleslaw

🥣 Prep Time: 10 mins
🕐 Total Time: 30 mins

Servings per Recipe: 10
Calories   184 kcal
Fat   12.6 g
Carbohydrates   16.1g
Protein   4 g
Cholesterol   0 mg
Sodium   514 mg

Ingredients

6 tbsp apple cider vinegar
6 tbsp vegetable oil
5 tbsp creamy peanut butter
3 tbsp soy sauce
3 tbsp brown sugar
2 tbsp minced fresh ginger root
1 1/2 tbsp minced garlic
5 C. thinly sliced green cabbage
2 C. thinly sliced red cabbage

2 C. shredded Napa cabbage
2 red bell peppers, thinly sliced
2 carrots, julienned
6 green onions, chopped
1/2 C. chopped fresh cilantro

Directions

1. In a medium bowl, add the vinegar, oil, peanut butter, soy sauce, brown sugar, ginger and garlic and beat till well combined.
2. In a large bowl, mix together the green cabbage, red cabbage, Napa cabbage, red bell peppers, carrots, green onions and cilantro.
3. Add the peanut butter mixture and toss to coat just before serving.

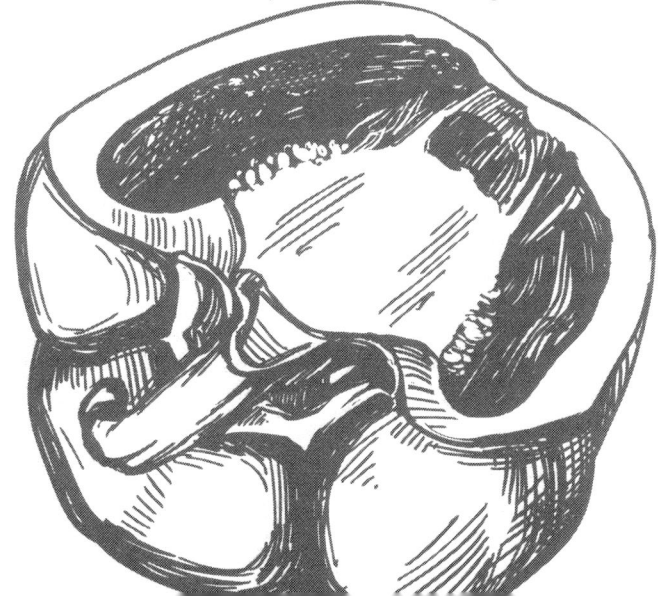

SUNFLOWER
Coleslaw

🥣 Prep Time: 15 mins
🕐 Total Time: 1 hr 15 mins

Servings per Recipe: 7
Calories   413 kcal
Fat   31.3 g
Carbohydrates   31.8g
Protein   4.6 g
Cholesterol   0 mg
Sodium   169 mg

Ingredients

1 C. olive oil
1/3 C. distilled white vinegar
1/2 C. white sugar
1 (3 oz.) package chicken flavored ramen noodles, crushed, seasoning packet reserved
1 large head fresh broccoli, diced

2 carrots, grated
2 bunches green onions, chopped
1 C. sunflower seeds

Directions

1. In a small bowl mix together the oil, vinegar, sugar and the seasoning packet from the ramen noodles and refrigerate for at least 1 hour before serving or overnight.
2. In a large bowl mix together the broccoli, carrots, green onions and sunflower seeds.
3. Crush the ramen noodles and stir in the salad mixture.
4. Place the dressing over salad and keep aside for about 10 minutes before serving.

Famous New England Coleslaw

Prep Time: 20 mins
Total Time: 8 hrs 20 mins

Servings per Recipe: 12
Calories   215 kcal
Fat   15.2 g
Carbohydrates   18.7g
Protein   3.2 g
Cholesterol   9 mg
Sodium   462 mg

Ingredients

1 head cabbage, cored and coarsely chopped
1 carrot, grated
1 sweet onion, minced
3 green onions, minced
1 dill pickle, minced
1 C. mayonnaise
2 C. buttermilk
2 tbsp dill pickle juice

2 tbsp vinegar
2 tbsp prepared yellow mustard
1/2 C. white sugar
1 pinch cayenne pepper
1 tsp salt, divided
1 clove garlic

Directions

1. In a large bowl, mix together the cabbage, carrot, sweet onion, green onions and dill pickle.
2. In another bowl, add the mayonnaise, buttermilk, dill pickle juice, vinegar, mustard, sugar, cayenne pepper and 3/4 tsp of the salt.
3. In a small bowl, add the remaining salt and garlic and mash well.
4. Add the mashed garlic into the dressing and beat well.
5. Place the dressing over the slaw and toss to coat.
6. Refrigerate, covered for about 8 hours or overnight before serving.

CHOCOLATE YOGURT
Cookies

🥣 Prep Time: 10 mins
🕐 Total Time: 22 mins

Servings per Recipe: 36
Calories   413 kcal
Fat   31.3 g
Carbohydrates   31.8 g
Protein   4.6 g
Cholesterol   0 mg
Sodium   169 mg

Ingredients

1/2 C. packed brown sugar
1/2 C. white sugar
1/4 C. margarine or butter
1/4 C. shortening
1/2 C. plain nonfat yogurt
2 tsps vanilla extract
1 3/4 C. all-purpose flour

1/2 tsp baking soda
1/2 tsp salt
2 C. semisweet chocolate chips

Directions

1. Coat some baking sheets with some oil then set your oven to 375 degrees before doing anything else.
2. Get a bowl, combine and cream the following: shortening, brown sugar, margarine, and white sugar. Stir the mix until it is fluffy then combine in the vanilla and yogurt.
3. Slowly work in the salt, baking soda, flour. Work the mix completely then add in the chocolate chips.
4. Layer dollops of the mix on the baking sheets and cook everything in the oven for 12 mins. Let the cookies cool completely then serve them.
5. Enjoy.

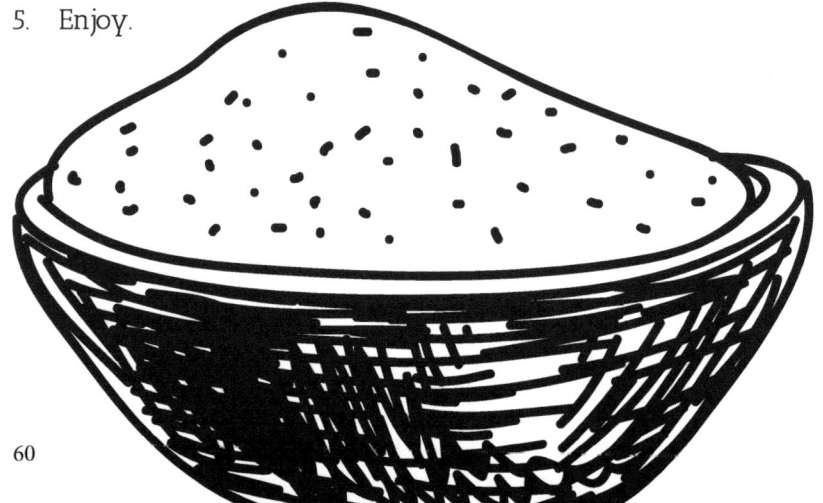

New England Apple Cookies

Prep Time: 30 mins
Total Time: 1 hr 18 mins

Servings per Recipe: 12
Calories   77 kcal
Fat   2.8 g
Carbohydrates   12.7g
Protein   0.9 g
Cholesterol   7 mg
Sodium   55 mg

Ingredients

- 2 C. all-purpose flour
- 1 tsp baking soda
- 1 tsp ground cinnamon
- 1 tsp ground cloves
- 1/2 tsp ground nutmeg
- 1/2 tsp salt
- 1/2 C. softened butter
- 1 1/2 C. packed brown sugar
- 1 egg, beaten
- 1 C. chopped walnuts
- 1 C. chopped apples
- 1 C. raisins
- 2/3 C. confectioners' sugar
- 1 tbsp milk

Directions

1. Set your oven to 350 degrees F before doing anything else and line the cookie sheets with parchment papers.
2. In a large bowl, sift together the flour, baking soda, spices and salt.
3. In another bowl, add the butter and beat till fluffy and light.
4. Add the egg and sugar and mix till well combined.
5. Add the egg mixture into the flour mixture and mix till well combined.
6. Fold in the apples, raisins and walnuts.
7. With a teaspoon, place the mixture onto the prepared cookie sheets in a single layer about 1 1/2-inches apart.
8. Cook everything in the oven for about 12-14 minutes.
9. Remove everything from the oven and keep aside on wire racks to cool completely.
10. Meanwhile for the glaze in a small bowl, mix together the remaining ingredients.
11. Pour the glaze over the cookies and serve.

CHEWY
Cookies 101

🥣 Prep Time: 20 mins
🕐 Total Time: 40 mins

Servings per Recipe: 36
Calories   90 kcal
Fat   5.4 g
Carbohydrates   9.4g
Protein   1.5 g
Cholesterol   10 mg
Sodium   50 mg

Ingredients

1 C. sifted all-purpose flour
1 tsp baking powder
1/2 tsp salt
1 tsp ground cinnamon
1/2 tsp ground nutmeg
1/2 C. shortening
3/4 C. white sugar
2 eggs

1 C. chopped walnuts
1 C. apples - peeled, cored and finely diced
1 C. rolled oats

Directions

1. Set your oven to 350 degrees F before doing anything else.
2. In a large bowl, mix together the flour, baking powder, cinnamon, nutmeg and salt.
3. In another bowl, add the shortening and white sugar and beat till smooth and creamy.
4. Add the eggs and beat till well combined.
5. Add the egg mixture into the flour mixture and mix till well combined.
6. Fold in the oats, apples and walnuts.
7. With a spoon, place the mixture onto the cookie sheets in a single layer about 2-inches apart.
8. Cook everything in the oven for about 12-15 minutes.
9. Remove everything from the oven and keep it all on wire racks to cool completely.

Quesadillas Tegucigalpa Style

Prep Time: 25 mins
Total Time: 2 hrs 10 mins

Servings per Recipe: 16
Calories	515 kcal
Fat	23.4 g
Carbohydrates	68g
Protein	9.9 g
Cholesterol	73 mg
Sodium	478 mg

Ingredients

- 1 1/2 C. margarine
- 3 C. white sugar
- 2 C. sifted all-purpose flour
- 1 C. rice flour
- 1 tbsp baking powder
- 6 room-temperature eggs
- 2 C. lukewarm milk
- 2 C. grated Parmesan cheese
- 1/2 C. white sugar
- 1/4 C. all-purpose flour
- 1/4 C. sesame seeds

Directions

1. Set your oven to 350 degrees F before doing anything else and lightly grease and flour a medium glass baking dish.
2. In a bowl, add the margarine and 3 C. of the sugar and beat till fluffy.
3. Add the eggs one at a time, mixing till well combined.
4. In another bowl, mix together 2 C. of the all-purpose flour, rice flour and baking powder.
5. Slowly, add the flour mixture into the egg mixture alternately with the milk, stirring well between each addition.
6. Slowly stir in the Parmesan cheese and transfer the mixture into the prepared baking dish.
7. In a small bowl, mix together 1/2 C. of the sugar, 1/4 C. of the all-purpose flour and sesame seeds.
8. Sprinkle evenly over the mixture in the baking dish.
9. Cook in the oven for about 45 minutes or till a toothpick inserted in the center comes out clean.
10. Cool completely and cut into squares.

TURKEY
Quesadillas

🥣 Prep Time: 10 mins
🕐 Total Time: 15 mins

Servings per Recipe: 6
Calories   141 kcal
Fat   5.9 g
Carbohydrates   11.6g
Protein   9.9 g
Cholesterol   26 mg
Sodium   165 mg

Ingredients

2 flour tortillas
1/2 C. shredded Cheddar cheese
1/4 lb. shredded cooked turkey meat
2 tbsp cranberry sauce
1/2 jalapeno pepper, seeded and minced
1 green onion, sliced
2 tbsp chopped fresh cilantro

Directions

1. Heat a skillet on medium heat and place 1 tortilla in the skillet.
2. Top with 1/2 of the Cheddar cheese, followed by turkey, cranberry sauce, jalapeño pepper, green onion and remaining Cheddar cheese.
3. Place the remaining tortilla over the top.
4. Cook for about 2-4 minutes per side.

American Quesadillas

🥣 Prep Time: 20 mins
🕐 Total Time: 38 mins

Servings per Recipe: 4
Calories   521 kcal
Fat   30 g
Carbohydrates   38.4g
Protein   24.4 g
Cholesterol   79 mg
Sodium   777 mg

Ingredients

1/2 lb. ground beef
1/2 red onion, diced
1 clove garlic, minced
1 pinch salt
1 C. shredded Cheddar cheese, divided
1/4 C. shredded mozzarella cheese
1 tbsp milk
1 tbsp butter, divided
2 (12 inch) flour tortillas

2 tbsp Thousand Island dressing, divided
1 romaine lettuce heart, sliced
1 tomato, sliced
1/2 red onion, sliced

Directions

1. Heat a large skillet and cook the beef, diced onion and garlic for about 5-8 minutes.
2. Stir in the salt and transfer the beef mixture into a pan on low heat.
3. Add 3/4 C. of the Cheddar cheese, mozzarella cheese and milk and Cook, stirring for about 3-5 minutes.
4. In a large skillet, melt half of the butter on medium heat and cook 1 tortilla for about 3 minutes.
5. Flip the tortilla and spread 1 tbsp dressing over the tortilla evenly.
6. Place half of the beef mixture over the tortilla and fold in half.
7. Cook for about 1-2 minutes per side.
8. Transfer into a serving plate.
9. Repeat with second tortilla.
10. Sprinkle the remaining 1/4 C. of the Cheddar cheese over the tortillas.
11. Keep aside to cool for about 5 minutes.
12. Cut into the wedges and serve with the lettuce, tomato and sliced onion.

BRIGHTLY FLAVORED
Quesadillas

🥘 Prep Time: 10 mins
🕐 Total Time: 30 mins

Servings per Recipe: 6
Calories   503 kcal
Fat   24.2 g
Carbohydrates   49.2g
Protein   23.2 g
Cholesterol   39 mg
Sodium   1421 mg

Ingredients

1 (15 oz.) can black beans, drained
1 tbsp vegetable oil
1/2 onion, chopped
1 red bell pepper, chopped
1 tsp chili powder
1 pinch cayenne pepper
1 pinch dried oregano
1 pinch dried basil
1 mango - peeled, seeded and diced
1 (6 oz.) package seasoned chicken-style vegetarian strips
6 (10 inch) flour tortillas

1 (8 oz.) package shredded Cheddar cheese
1 C. arugula leaves
1 (4 oz.) jar jalapeno pepper rings (optional)
1 (8 oz.) jar salsa

Directions

1. In a pan, place the beans on medium heat and cook for about 5 minutes.
2. With a potato masher, mash the beans partially.
3. Reduce the heat to low and keep warm until ready to serve.
4. In a skillet, heat the oil on medium heat and sauté the onion, red bell pepper, chili powder, cayenne pepper, oregano and basil till tender.
5. Stir in the mango and vegetarian chicken strips and cook for about 2 minutes.
6. Heat another skillet on medium heat and cook the tortillas for about 2 minutes per side.
7. Place the black beans over warm tortillas, followed by the mango mixture, Cheddar cheese, arugula and jalapeño.
8. Fold the tortillas over the filling and top with the salsa to serve.

Milanese Quesadillas

Prep Time: 20 mins
Total Time: 50 mins

Servings per Recipe: 5
Calories   880 kcal
Fat   46.2 g
Carbohydrates   65.6g
Protein   49.6 g
Cholesterol   121 mg
Sodium   2178 mg

Ingredients

- 1 lb. thinly sliced chicken breast meat
- 1/2 tsp salt
- 1/2 tsp ground black pepper
- 2 tbsp olive oil
- 14 slices precooked turkey bacon, chopped
- 1 (8 oz.) package sliced fresh mushrooms
- 1 C. Alfredo sauce
- 1 tsp butter
- 5 large flour tortillas
- 2 C. shredded mozzarella cheese

Directions

1. Sprinkle the chicken with the salt and black pepper.
2. In a large skillet, heat the olive oil on medium heat and cook the chicken for about 8-10 minutes.
3. Remove the chicken from the skillet and keep aside.
4. Discard any excess grease from the pan.
5. In the same skillet, add the bacon and mushrooms on medium heat and cook for about 5 minutes.
6. Reduce the heat to low.
7. Cut the chicken into bite-size strips.
8. Add the Alfredo sauce and chicken strips into the skillet and simmer for a few minutes.
9. In another skillet, melt the butter and place a tortilla in the melted butter.
10. Place about 1/5 of the chicken Alfredo mixture onto 1 half of warm tortilla.
11. Sprinkle about 1/5 of the mozzarella cheese over the chicken alfredo mixture.
12. Fold the tortilla in half and cook for about 3-5 minutes.
13. Carefully flip the quesadilla and cook for about 3-5 minutes.
14. Repeat with the remaining tortillas and filling.
15. Slice the quesadillas into thirds to serve.

CAJUN Burgers with Lemon Sauce

Prep Time: 10 mins
Total Time: 15 mins

Servings per Recipe: 4
Calories   246.9
Fat   6.5g
Cholesterol   56.6mg
Sodium   1130.1mg
Carbohydrates   35.9g
Protein   112.8g

Ingredients

1 (15 ounce) cans cannellini beans (drain liquid) or 1 (15 ounce) cans chickpeas (drain liquid)
1 egg
1 onion
1/2 C. breadcrumbs, crushed crackers or flour
1 tbsp minced garlic
Salt and pepper
1 tbsp cumin (optional)
Nonstick cooking spray
Curry powder
Garam masala

Smoked paprika
Minced chipotle pepper
Cayenne
Oregano
Cajun seasoning
Cheese
1/4 C. mayonnaise
2 -3 tbsps lemon juice
1 tbsp garlic powder or 1 tbsp minces garlic
1 chipotle pepper, minced (optional)

Directions

1. Get a small bowl: Add the sauce ingredients. Whisk them well. Place the sauce in the fridge.
2. Get a food processor: Add the garlic, onion bean and seasonings mix. Pulse them several times until they become finely chopped.
3. Add the breadcrumbs with egg and flour. Mix them well. Shape the mix into 4 burgers.
4. Place a large skillet on medium heat. Heat the sesame oil in it. Add the burgers and cook them for 8 min on each side. Assemble your burgers with the lemon sauce and your favorite toppings.
5. Serve them right away.
6. Enjoy.

Kalamata Feta Burgers

Prep Time: 25 mins
Total Time: 50 mins

Servings per Recipe: 4
Calories   318 kcal
Fat   21.9 g
Carbohydrates   3.6 g
Protein   25.5 g
Cholesterol   123 mg
Sodium   800 mg

Ingredients
1 lb ground turkey
1 C. crumbled feta cheese
1/2 C. Kalamata olives, pitted and sliced
2 tsps dried oregano
Ground black pepper to taste

Directions
1. Before you do anything preheat the grill.
2. Get a large mixing bowl: Add the turkey, feta cheese, olives, oregano, and pepper then combine them well. Shape the mix into 4 cakes.
3. Grill the burger cakes for 7 min on each side. Assemble your burgers with your favorite toppings.
4. Enjoy.

HOT ICEBERG
Chicken Burgers

🥣 Prep Time: 20 mins
🕐 Total Time: 35 mins

Servings per Recipe: 4
Calories   374 kcal
Fat   8.8 g
Carbohydrates   25.3g
Protein   45.5 g
Cholesterol   111 mg
Sodium   1111 mg

Ingredients

- 1/4 C. light sour cream
- 1/4 C. reduced fat blue cheese crumbles
- 1/4 tsp Worcestershire sauce
- 1 1/2 lbs ground chicken
- 1/4 C. hot pepper sauce
- 1/2 tsp celery salt (optional)
- 1/4 tsp poultry seasoning
- 1/2 tsp paprika
- 1 pinch cayenne pepper, or to taste
- 1 tbsp hot pepper sauce
- 4 Kaiser Rolls split
- 4 leaves iceberg lettuce
- 1/2 C. diced celery

Directions

1. Before you do anything preheat the grill.
2. To make the sauce:
3. Get a mixing bowl: Add the sour cream, blue cheese, and Worcestershire sauce then mix them well. Place it aside.
4. Get a large mixing bowl: chicken, 1/4 C. hot sauce, celery salt, poultry seasoning, paprika, and cayenne pepper, black pepper and salt. Mix them well.
5. Shape the mix into 4 burger cakes. Grill them for 8 min. Flip the burger cakes and brush the upper side with 1 tsp of the hot sauce for each. Cook them for 7 min on the other side.
6. Assemble your burgers with 1 lettuce leaf, 2 tbsps of cheese sauce and 2 tbsps of celery per each burger. Serve them right away.
7. Enjoy.

Sesame Burgers

Prep Time: 30 mins
Total Time: 1 h

Servings per Recipe: 4
Calories	186.4
Fat	3.0g
Cholesterol	0.0mg
Sodium	352.6mg
Carbohydrates	29.4g
Protein	11.9g

Ingredients

- 1 (15 ounce) cans cannellini, rinsed and drained
- 1/3 C. chopped onion
- 2 garlic cloves, peeled
- 1 tbsp fresh parsley, chopped
- 2 tbsps nutritional yeast
- 2 tbsps sesame seeds
- 2 egg whites
- 1/2 C. breadcrumbs
- 1 tsp paprika
- 1/2 tsp sea salt
- 1/2 tsp black pepper
- 1 dash cayenne pepper

Directions

1. Wash the beans with some fresh water. Place it in a colander to get remove the water.
2. Get a food processor: Add the beans with rest of the ingredients. Pulse them several times until they become smooth. Transfer the mix into a bowl and cover it.
3. Place it in the fridge for 45 min. Shape the mix into 4 burgers.
4. Place a large skillet on medium heat. Heat the sesame oil in it. Add the burgers and cook them for 8 min on each side. Assemble your burgers with your favorite toppings.
5. Serve them right away.
6. Enjoy.

FETA
Spinach Burgers

🥣 Prep Time: 15 mins
🕐 Total Time: 25 mins

Servings per Recipe: 8
Calories   331 kcal
Fat   16.3 g
Carbohydrates   17g
Protein   28.7 g
Cholesterol   123 mg
Sodium   583 mg

Ingredients

2 lbs ground turkey
1 1/2 C. fresh bread crumbs
1 1/2 C. chopped baby spinach
1/2 C. light Greek dressing
5 oz. feta cheese, cubed
1/4 large onion, finely chopped

1 egg
Salt and ground black pepper to taste

Directions

1. Before you do anything preheat the grill.
2. Get a mixing bowl: Add all the ingredients. Mix them well. Shape the mix into 8 burger cakes. Grill them for 8 min on each side.
3. Assemble your burgers with your favorite toppings.
4. Enjoy.

Feta Spinach Burgers

Bell Artichoke Burgers

Prep Time: 15 mins
Total Time: 25 mins

Servings per Recipe: 6
Calories	299.1
Fat	4.0g
Cholesterol	0.0mg
Sodium	673.8mg
Carbohydrates	55.4g
Protein	112.3g

Ingredients

2 (15 ounce) cans garbanzo beans, drained and rinsed
1 small onion, chopped
6 garlic cloves, chopped
1/2 C. red bell pepper, chopped
1/3 C. Kalamata olive, chopped
1 (8 ounce) jars marinated artichokes, drained and chopped
2 C. spinach, chopped (fresh)
1/2 C. oats
1/2 tsp dried oregano
1/4 tsp salt
1/4 tsp pepper
1/2 C. breadcrumbs

Directions

1. Get a mixing bowl: Add the beans, onion, and garlic. Press them with a fork and mash them for a bit. Stir in the remaining ingredients and mix them well.
2. Shape the mix into 6 burgers. Place a large skillet on medium heat and grease it. Cook in it the burgers for 6 min on each side.
3. Assemble your burgers with your favorite toppings. Serve them right away.
4. Enjoy.

FATHIA'S Favorite

🥣 Prep Time: 15 mins
🕐 Total Time: 35 mins

Servings per Recipe: 4
Calories   272 kcal
Fat   17.7 g
Carbohydrates   3.7g
Protein   23.5 g
Cholesterol   124 mg
Sodium   222 mg

Ingredients
1 lb ground beef
1/2 onion, finely chopped
1 egg, beaten
1 tsp hot pepper sauce (e.g. Tabasco(TM))
1 tbsp dry bread crumbs
1 tsp paprika
1 tsp dried parsley
Salt and pepper to taste

1/3 C. shredded Monterey Jack cheese
1/2 fresh red chili pepper, finely chopped
4 slices pickled jalapeno pepper, finely chopped

Directions
1. Before you do anything preheat the oven to 350 F.
2. Get a large mixing bowl: Add the beef, onion, egg, hot pepper sauce, and bread crumbs, paprika, parsley, salt, and pepper. Mix them well.
3. Get a mixing bowl: Add the cheese, red chili pepper, and jalapeno pepper. Mix them well to make the stuffing.
4. Shape the mix into 4 burger cakes then press them flat. Place the cheese mix in the middle of each patty and pull the meat mix around it to cover it.
5. Press the burger patties slightly. Place them on a lined up baking sheet. Cook it in the oven for 11 min. Flip the patties and cook them for another 11 min.
6. Assemble your burgers with your favorite toppings.
7. Enjoy.

Chili Corn Burgers

🥣 Prep Time: 5 mins
⏲ Total Time: 25 mins

Servings per Recipe: 8
Calories   124.7
Fat   1.0g
Cholesterol   0.0mg
Sodium   586.3mg
Carbohydrates   25.8g
Protein   5.0g

Ingredients

1 carrot, sliced
1 (15 ounce) cans garbanzo beans
2 C. store-brand fresh salsa
1 C. crushed corn flakes
1/2 C. whole wheat flour
1/2 tsp fresh pepper

Salt
1 pinch chili powder

Directions

1. Fill 1/4 inch of a bowl with water. Add the carrot. Cook it in the microwave for 3 min. discard the water.
2. Get a mixing bowl: Add the beans with carrot. Press them with a fork until they become finely mashed. Add the salsa with corn flakes, flour, salt, chili powder and pepper. Mix them well.
3. Shape the mix into 8 burgers. Grease a skillet and put it on medium heat. Add the burgers and cook them for 9 min on each side.
4. Assemble your burgers with your favorite toppings. Serve them right away.
5. Enjoy.

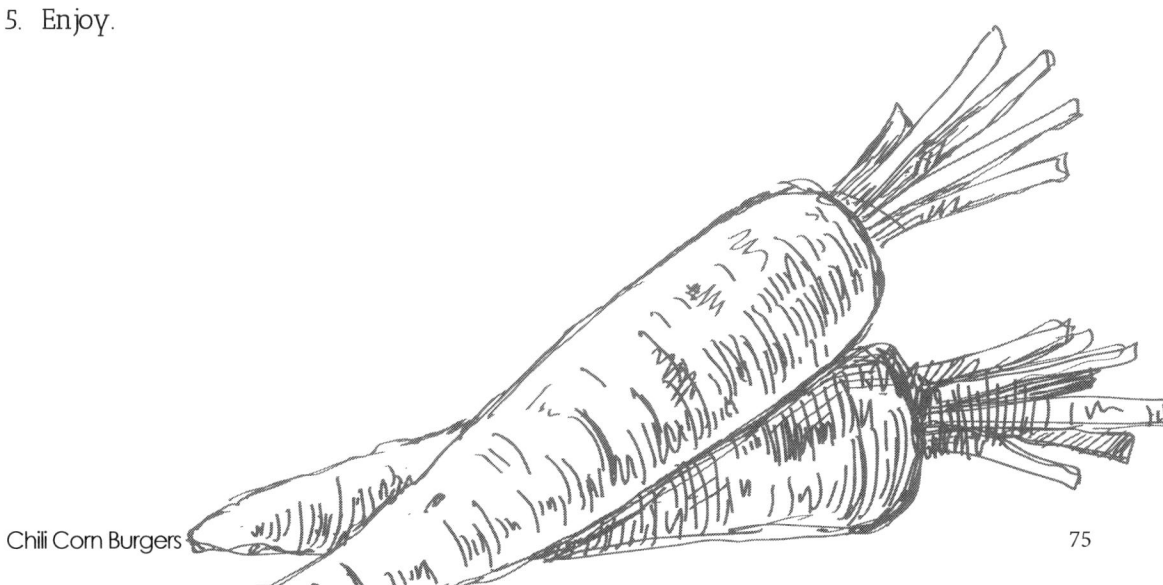

ITALIAN BALSAMIC Mushroom Burger

🥣 Prep Time: 30 mins
🕐 Total Time: 55 mins

Servings per Recipe: 8
Calories   778 kcal
Fat   43.5 g
Carbohydrates   41.1g
Protein   53.7 g
Cholesterol   232 mg
Sodium   1386 mg

Ingredients

- 8 slices turkey bacon
- 1/2 white onion, diced
- 1 clove garlic, minced
- 1 tbsp balsamic vinegar, or to taste
- 5 fresh mushrooms, chopped
- 1/2 lb ground beef
- 1/2 C. dry bread crumbs
- 1 tsp Italian seasoning
- 1 1/2 tbsps grated Parmesan cheese
- 1 egg
- Salt and pepper to taste
- 1 malted wheat hamburger bun, split in half
- 2 slices tomato
- 2 slices Swiss cheese

Directions

1. Before you do anything preheat the oven to 375 F.
2. Place a large skillet on medium heat. Add the bacon and cook it until it becomes crunchy. Drain it and place it aside.
3. Add the garlic with onion to the bacon grease in the skillet. Cook them for 4 min on medium heat. Stir in the balsamic vinegar then cook them for 1 min.
4. Stir in the mushroom and cook them for 4 min. turn off the heat. Chop the 4 cooked bacon strips.
5. Get a mixing bowl: Add the chopped bacon, ground beef, bread crumbs, Italian seasoning, Parmesan cheese, mushroom mix and egg, salt and pepper. Combine them well.
6. Shape the mix into 2 burgers. Place the burgers on the bottom sandwich buns then top them with tomato, 2 strips of the bacon and one slice of Swiss cheese.
7. Cover the burgers with the upper buns. Serve your burgers right away.
8. Enjoy.

Birdie Burgers

🥣 Prep Time: 5 mins
⏲ Total Time: 0 mins

Servings per Recipe: 6
Calories   479 kcal
Fat   27.2 g
Carbohydrates   25.2g
Protein   31.5 g
Cholesterol   96 mg
Sodium   467 mg

Ingredients
1 1/2 lbs lean ground beef
1 C. Birds Eye(R) Recipe Ready Chopped Onions & Garlic
6 slices Cheddar cheese
6 hamburger buns
Lettuce leaves

Directions
1. Before you do anything preheat the grill.
2. Get a mixing bowl: Add the beef and Recipe Ready Chopped Onions, Garlic, salt and pepper. Mix them well. Form them into 6 burgers.
3. Cook them in the grill for 7 min on each side. Assemble your burgers with cheddar cheese slices and lettuce leaves. Serve them right away.
4. Enjoy.